Secrets of Leadership
—Insights From the Panchatantra

Luis S.R. Vas
Anita S.R. Vas

PUSTAK MAHAL®
Delhi•Bangalore•Mumbai•Patna•Hyderabad•London

Publishers
Pustak Mahal®, Delhi

J-3/16 , Daryaganj, New Delhi-110002
☎ 23276539, 23272783, 23272784 • *Fax:* 011-23260518
E-mail: info@pustakmahal.com • *Website:* www.pustakmahal.com

London Office
5, Roddell Court, Bath Road, Slough SL3 OQJ, England
E-mail: pustakmahaluk@pustakmahal.com

Sales Centre
10-B, Netaji Subhash Marg, Daryaganj, New Delhi-110002
☎ 23268292, 23268293, 23279900 • *Fax:* 011-23280567
E-mail: rapidexdelhi@indiatimes.com

Branch Offices
Bangalore: ☎ 22234025
E-mail: pmblr@sancharnet.in • pustak@sancharnet.in
Mumbai: ☎ 22010941
E-mail: rapidex@bom5.vsnl.net.in
Patna: ☎ 3294193 • *Telefax:* 0612-2302719
E-mail: rapidexptn@rediffmail.com
Hyderabad: *Telefax:* 040-24737290
E-mail: pustakmahalhyd@yahoo.co.in

© **Pustak Mahal, Delhi**

ISBN 978-81-223-0802-0

Edition : 2007

Printed at : Param Offsetters, Okhla, New Delhi-110020

Contents _____

Introduction

" "F"ar from being merely a collection of children's stories as it is generally supposed to be, the Panchatantra is a very pragmatic, extremely useful guidebook to the art of practical living," so begins the announcement of a workshop on *The Panchatantra as a Guide For Living*. "It is the world's oldest how-to-succeed book. It has a realistic grasp of life that has never been equalled or surpassed. As a guidebook for leaders, and as a resource for the perplexed, the Panchatantra exhibits an eternal relevance. It is free of all cant and hypocrisy. It relishes life and considers living to be an art that requires the right attitude as well as the proper training. In this Workshop, the Panchatantra is appraised for its continuing relevance and the lessons that can be profitably learnt from it. Its philosophy is simple, germane and never piously impractical, but it never deviates from an ethical approach to all of life's problems."

The Workshop announcement then proceeds to describe how it proposes to use the Panchatantra to solve your problems at work and in life.

This is not a gimmick. The Panchatantra is a work relevant for all times whether it is used in a Management Workshop or as a general guide to daily living. Leadership is involved in both.

Through a jungle of speaking animals, a sage, Vishnu Sharma, created a storehouse of wisdom in the form of short stories for children as well as adults. These stories, written as far back as 2,000 years ago, came to be known as *Panchatantra*. The influence of Vishnu Sharma's stories has been vast. By the 3rd and 4th centuries, the Panchatantra had already been translated into Syriac and Arabic from the original version in Sanskrit written in the 1st and 2nd centuries AD.

Subsequently, there were versions in Paisachi, Pahlavi and Prakrit (other Indian languages). The Panchatantra has been translated into

50 different languages in some 200 different versions. What is interesting is that even Grimm's fairy tales can be traced back to this treasure-house of animal tales created by Vishnu Sharma.

There is, however, a lesser-known version that, as a school of thought, claims to be the original and credits the authorship to Vasubhagabhatta. The genesis of this version lies in mythology — that Lord Shiva told the stories to Parvati, his consort, which were overheard by Pashpadatta, who was born on earth as Gunadya and was appointed as a noble laureate in the court of an emperor named Salivahara. Gunadya then retold these stories in Paisachi and the compilation of his stories is called *Brahatkatham* (ocean of stories). Vasubhaga drew a few stories from them and compiled them into what is known as *Panchatantra*.

Vasubhaga's Panchatantra has found mention in the Javanese, Laotian and Siamese versions, in addition to a few Indian versions as well.

Coming back to Vishnu Sharma, how he wrote these stories is a story in itself. The preface of the Panchatantra tells us that there was once a king called Amarshakti. He had three sons – Bahushakti, Ugrashakti and Anantshakti – all dullards. Amarshakti despaired. "Show me a way to educate them," he told his courtiers. One amongst them was a wise man named Sumati. He came up with the idea that the princes should not be taught the scriptures but only the wisdom in them. There is a man called Vishnu Sharma, he said, who could do just this.

Vishnu Sharma was summoned. He asked for just six months to make the princes wise. Disbelieving, Amarshakti watched as the miracle began.

Letting his imagination take flight, Vishnu Sharma guided it and the princes into a world where myth was turned into reality. Weaving one story into another, the aspect under consideration was amply illustrated and elaborated. The princes were exposed to life through the lesson or moral that each situation taught.

Panchatantra means *five devices* or *treatises* — (*pancha* = five, *tantra* = devices or treatises). The stories under five different heads cover all aspects of management, personal life and cunning that one has to combat in life. The first of the Panchatantra deals with *Mitrabhed* (rift between friends), which illustrates a situation where friends are separated by a cunning third person.

Mitrabhed begins with the story of a bull. Stranded in a forest, he lives in constant fear of wild animals. But the lion king of the forest is in awe of the bull's voice and figure. The two are brought together by Damanak. Damanak and Karkat are the two foxes attending to the king. The bull and the lion become friends. The bull is wise and learned and soon the lion too acquires a lot of knowledge. The bull teaches him the laws of city life as opposed to the jungle laws. Soon the lion stops hunting.

This grieves Damanak and Karkat, for they used to feed on the lion's hunt. So Damanak starts driving a wedge between the two friends. He tells the bull that the lion is after all a carnivore and that he is planning to kill him, the bull, the next day. He then tells the lion that he has heeded the herbivore for too long and now that he has forgotten how to hunt, the bull is planning to kill him. Damanak tells many stories to illustrate his point and the friends slowly begin to fall into his trap.

Subsidiary to this theme are stories underlining the different ways of reducing the enemy's strength. If the enemy is very strong, the intellect should take over, which is illustrated in the story of the lion and the rabbit. And if the enemy is mighty, then a clever plan has to be worked out first. The enemy could be anybody — a poisonous snake, a mighty king or even the invincible ocean.

Friends and their acquisition is the section called *Mitrasamprapti*. The story of the pigeons caught in a net is illustrative of *Mitrasamprapti*.

7

Together the pigeons fly off with the net to Hiranyak, the mouse. The mouse bites through the net and sets the birds free. In addition, there are stories which stress the need for courage. A coward, says Vishnu Sharma, would not be able to enjoy himself even when good fortune smiles upon him. *It is courage and amity that saved the life of four friends* – the raven, the mouse, the tortoise and the deer.

Pragmatism is, however, important for you to emerge a survivor as the Panchatantra wishes you to be. So the section on worldly wisdom, *Kakolukiyam*, describes the ways of the world. *Trust not everybody,* warns Vishnu Sharma, *especially those who having been enemies, now pretend friendship.* Nip it in the bud; all is fair in war; a king should never run away from war – these are some of the other lessons. In modern terms, translate war into the competition we all face in life. The moral in Panchatantra stories, therefore, is in sharp contrast to our conventional understanding of the word 'moral'. They are not comforting stories about the victory of good over evil. Nor do they preach conventional ethics. They comprise a complete life management manual – dealing with all aspects of one's life in the complex and varied world in which we live.

The lessons learnt are applicable equally to modern man's life and work as to the princes for whom the Panchatantra was originally devised. They try to expose the reader to various situations that he could come across in his daily life and prepare him to face them with courage and prudence.

Dropping names can be beneficial, says Vishnu Sharma. There was once a forest in which all the lakes had dried up due to drought. A herd of elephants living in the forest began dying of thirst. Their king then led them to a faraway lake, which was at a lower level. The elephants were happy. But around the lake was a warren of rabbits. Each time the elephants visited the lake many young rabbits were trampled over. Distressed, the rabbits hit upon a plan. A representative from them went to the elephants and said the moon was unhappy that the elephants were drinking water from the moon's own lake. Paying their obeisance to the reflection of the moon in the lake, the elephants went back never to return to that lake!

Labdhapranasha or *the slip betwixt the cup and lip* is illustrated by the story of the crocodile and the monkey. They become friends and the monkey gives the crocodile some jamuns everyday. One day the crocodile takes some for his wife. The wife is thrilled. If the jamun is so sweet, the heart of the monkey who feeds on them should be sweeter, she reasons. She wants to eat the monkey's heart or else she'll lay down her life, she says.

The crocodile is in a fix but eventually invites the monkey home for a meal. Carrying him on his back he reaches the middle of the lake and then tells the monkey about his wife's intentions. The monkey immediately responds appropriately and succeeds in saving his life.

Other stories relate how that which is acquired undeservedly is bound to be lost; how a beautiful woman can rob a man of his senses; how believing flattery can harm; and how inconsistent behaviour should always be watched as in the story of the old Brahmin whose young wife suddenly turned over-affectionate towards him. Later, he discovered he'd lost her to a young lover.

Throughout the book, there is no flattering reference to women. Women, says Vishnu Sharma, are always unfaithful, and a beautiful woman? She cannot be satiated by any number of lovers! A woman who does not please her husband is no woman at all and a man who is always trying to please a woman is sure to face doom. Does this explain why male chauvinism was so deeply rooted in ancient times?

The concluding section is called *Aparikshitakaraka* or *that which has not yet been tried*. Any new situation demands that it is fully considered for its pros and cons before any action is taken. What happened to the four friends, three of whom were well versed in the Scriptures? In an attempt to put to use their knowledge they brought to life a dead lion not heeding the fourth man's advice, which was based on sound common sense... and reaped the consequences. *Book knowledge alone is not enough, the moral emphasises; application is essential.*

Vishnu Sharma's tales are universal in their appeal. Though much of the conversation is put into the mouths of beasts, it is genuine human feeling and intelligence that prompts the utterances. The original has page after page of shrewd observations, proverbs and well-worn maxims. Vishnu Sharma aimed at nothing less than teaching worldly wisdom to be obtained by the exercise of intelligence in securing a moderate fortune, personal safety, learning and a wide circle of friends – in a word, happiness through leadership.

This faraway land where fantasy dissolves into the factual has entertained children and adults all over the world. The crescendo is reached with Vishnu Sharma's claim that you are not helpless in any situation, not even when faced by Lord Indra, the King of the Heavens. What more does one need to be happy?

The *Hitopadesha* (Good Advice) is an independent version of the Panchatantra, in a more elegant style than the Panchatantra. This simple recast of the Panchatantra is most popular among beginners in Sanskrit.

The Panchatantra is divided into five volumes:
1. Rift between friends
2. The winning of friends
3. Untrustworthy friendship of a former enemy
4. Presence of mind
5. Untested situations

The First Tantra *(Mitrabhed)*

Rift Between Friends: The first tantra begins with the story of two friends (a lion and a bullock). A greedy jackal creates differences between them by employing evil means. All the other stories of this section are interrelated and follow in a sequential manner.

The Second Tantra *(Mitrasamprapti)*

The Winning of Friends: The second tantra begins with a story of Chitragreeva, the pigeon and Hiranyak, the mouse. The intelligent mouse helps Chitragreeva in releasing himself along with other pigeons from the net of a fowler. *This section sheds light on the importance of friendship and teamwork among like-minded people of varied talents.*

The Third Tantra *(Kakolukiyam)*

The Friendship of a Former Enemy is Untrustworthy: The third tantra stresses one should beware of a friend who was formerly an enemy.

The Fourth Tantra *(Labdhapranasha)*

Presence of Mind Particularly During Emergencies: The fourth tantra underlines *the importance of a man's presence of mind during emergencies.*

The Fifth Tantra *(Aparikshitakaraka)*

Accomplishment of One's Task Using Discriminative Intelligence: The fifth tantra explains *the importance of discriminative intelligence in the accomplishment of one's task in untested situations.*

In this collection of Panchatantra stories, we have tried to show what bearing these fables have on our leadership skills. We have highlighted some of the morals embedded in the fables themselves (in italicised letters) as well as provided whatever modern insights possible from them at the end of each story (in italicised letters within rules). We have also occasionally provided relevant observations. You are encouraged to draw your own insights from these classic tales of wisdom.

In the Conclusion, we have stated the five leadership secrets of the Panchatantra as revealed in the five tantras and combined them with a typical modern management plan designed to bring your newly-learnt leadership skills to fruition.

We would appreciate receiving your feedback via e-mail. Our e-mail ID is given below.

We dedicate this book to India's future leaders.

Luis S.R. Vas
Anita S.R. Vas
vasluis@hotmail.com

11

The First Tantra – Mitrabhed

Rift Between Friends

On an auspicious day and at an auspicious moment, Vishnu Sharma began the education of the princes. He began with a tale of a bull, which was abandoned by its master in a dense forest.

There was a city named Mahilaropya in southern India. In this city lived a pious merchant named Vardhamaan. One night, when Vardhamaan was about to sleep, a thought suddenly came to haunt his mind that he might lose all his wealth. Then even his family members would abandon him. All night long, Vardhamaan kept thinking about various ways to earn more wealth. At last, he concluded that commerce was the only way to earn money with honour.

In the morning, Vardhamaan packed many utensils and pots on a bullock cart and set out for Mathura along with a caravan of fellow traders. He was intending to sell the utensils in the city of Mathura. Two oxen, Mandak and Sanjeevak, were hauling the bullock cart. When the caravan reached the dense forest, Sanjeevak got stuck in marshy land and broke one of his legs. The accident caused Vardhamaan great anguish. His love for the bullock made him stay with the animal for three nights. Seeing Vardhamaan's plight, his friends said: "This forest is inhabited by tigers and lions. You are risking our lives also along with this ox. Do not worry about the ox and leave it here. Believe us, it will recover in a few days or die. But in any case, you cannot help it."

Vardhamaan agreed with his friends and appointed some guards to protect the bullock and resumed his journey. After a while, the guards got tired of keeping watch on a seemingly useless animal. So they deserted Sanjeevak and went to join Vardhamaan. They falsely told him that the ox had died and they had performed the last rites. Vardhamaan was sorry to hear the news, but accepted it as God's will.

In the forest, however, fresh green grass, pure air and cool river water had a transforming effect on Sanjeevak. It recovered and regained its health once again. In fact, it was even stronger than before. Bristling with energy, Sanjeevak began to rub its horns against the heap of sand and made all sorts of calls.

A lion named Pingalak also inhabited the forest. One day, Pingalak came to quench his thirst in the river Yamuna. Incidentally, he heard the bellowing of the bull Sanjeevak and mistook it for some ferocious animal. The bellowing had actually frightened the lion! So he hid behind some bushes under a banyan tree. The lion Pingalak had two jackals as his ministers. They always followed the lion everywhere. Their names were Damanak and Karkat. The frightened behaviour of Pingalak surprised them. They began to discuss this behaviour.

Damanak asked Karkat: "Why did the lion hide?" Karkat however cautioned him against meddling in the matters of their king and said they should not think about things that did not concern them.

A person who unnecessarily meddles with matters not relevant to him is destroyed in the same way the monkey was killed while removing the wedge, said Karkat.

Damanak requested Karkat to tell him the tale of the monkey.

13

The Tale of the Monkey

The construction of a temple was on outside a town. Near the site, a huge wooden log was being split. At lunch, the workers fixed a wedge between the split wood and went for a bite. A monkey had been watching the activities of the workers since morning. When the workers were away, the monkey descended from the tree and began to meddle with the log of wood. During his play, he noticed the wedge and began to withdraw it. But he forgot that his tail was hanging between the split ends of the log. As soon as the wedge was out, the

split ends closed squeezing the tail of the monkey. The monkey tried hard to free himself, but in vain. No help was available nearby. By the time the workers returned from their lunch, the monkey was dead.

Modern Insight: It is advisable not to interfere in the affairs of strangers, your elders and superiors, since, lacking their experience and knowledge, you will only succeed in antagonising rather than helping them, if that was your intention. In the process, you could also harm yourself.

Karkat said that if an inferior person advises a king without being asked to, he is always dishonoured. That is why one should consider the situation, think and only then speak.

Damanak argued that even inferior people become superior when they serve the king. On the contrary, superior people who do not guide the king become inferior. A king trusts all people around him even though they might be uncultured, uneducated and ignorant. Even servants, who constantly show concern for the causes and reasons behind a king's happiness and sorrow, are slowly upgraded to a higher position by a grateful king. Those people who think that it requires a lot of penance and hard work to please a king are in fact lethargic and stupid.

If one can train animals like snakes, elephants and lions using different methods, it doesn't need great effort for wise people to control a king.

Karkat asked Damanak what he wanted to do. Damanak said, "Today, our king along with his family is scared and terrified. We should therefore go to him and inquire about the cause of his terror."

Karkat inquired, "How does one know whether the king is terrified or not?"

Damanak replied: "What is so great about knowing that? *It is said that even an animal can understand spoken commands. With inspiration, a horse can bear the weight on an elephant and wise people can understand even unspoken things.*

"One can understand the feelings of a person on the basis of the following things: hints, thinking, actions, speech, eyes and facial expressions. That is the reason why I shall approach the terrified king and, using my intellect, appease him and regain the post of minister once again."

Karkat said: "You don't even know what service is, how shall you serve the king then?"

Damanak replied: "I am well acquainted with principles of service. When I was a child, sitting on my father's lap I heard practical rules of wisdom from saints.

"People who don't recognise an individual's merit should not serve the king because it is like ploughing a barren field and one is sure not to get any produce from it at all.

"It is still good to serve the king even if he lacks wealth and powers because doing so one reaps the fruits of his service in future.

"Wise people should never think of material gains from an ignorant king in return for their service.

15

"Those who criticise the king should be their own critics first, because either they are not fit for service or not aware of the rules to serve. The servant should pay due respect to the queen, the prince, the princess, the chief minister, the priest and the sentries of the royal palace as well.

"He who always greets the king and knows his dos and don'ts well and acts accordingly is a beloved of the king. One who stands at the forefront in battle, walks behind the king in the city and waits at the door of the royal chamber is loved by the king."

Karkat asked, "What shall you say first to the king when you approach him?"

Damanak said: "When the rain is good, a seed germinates and grows into a tree and from the tree many more seeds take birth. In the same way, one tale gives birth to another tale and so on. I shall, therefore, not talk about his bad times because even the Lord feels insulted by talk that highlights unhappy events which haunt him."

With these words, Damanak proceeded towards Pingalak. When the king saw Damanak arriving, he instructed the guard to let him in, for Damanak was the son of his former minister. The lion king was pleased to see him. Very respectfully, Damanak said: "Although my visit appears purposeless, but all the inferior as well as superior people find a purpose to visit the king."

Pingalak said, "Let us keep this discussion aside. I have allowed you in because you are the son of my former minister. I do not know whether you are capable or incapable, so please speak openly and express what you desire."

Damanak responded, "The king shouldn't express even a menial task in court. If you intend to listen to my desire, you may hear it in privacy."

Insight: A secret heard by six ears is easily spread. A secret heard by four ears remains a secret. That is why a prudent king – or any other person – should perform his tasks in such a way that six ears don't even hear a whisper of it.

In privacy, Damanak asked Pingalak: "Why did you hide that day while you were drinking water in the river?"

Pingalak replied: "Didn't you hear the strange roar and bellowing. It seems that some dangerous animal has come in the forest. I intend to abandon this forest for life."

Damanak said: "Is it right for a king like you to run away just on listening to loud bellowing? It could possibly be noise from drums or anything else. That is the reason why one should not fear noise, like Gomayu."

Pingalak asked in surprise: "What do you mean?"

The Story of Gomayu

Once, a jackal named Gomayu felt very hungry and was roaming the forest in search of food. Suddenly, he stumbled upon a battlefield where two armies were standing face to face ready for war. Just then, a branch of a tree struck the drum that had fallen besides the tree and this produced a loud sound. The sound frightened the jackal to such an extent that he began to worry about his life. He thought: 'I think I'll now be destroyed. Before the creature who is making such a loud sound sees me, I should run away from here.'

Then the thought entered his mind that it was not right for him to abandon the forest where his ancestors had lived. So, Gomayu decided to investigate the cause of the sound first.

Very cautiously, Gomayu moved ahead. He went near the drum and curiously began playing with it himself. He thought he had found

much food after many days. There would definitely be plenty of meat beneath the skin. Thinking so, he made a hole in the drum and shoved his paw into it. But as the skin of the drum was torn apart, it turned out to be empty with no trace of meat inside!

"Without proper knowledge, one should not jump to conclusions on merely hearing some sound. A king who does not lose courage while fighting a formidable enemy shall never be vanquished."

Insight: With effort and self-control, you can learn to retain your wits in difficult situations; soon, you will master control and come out a winner, a leader and a happier person in life.

"That is why we should first find out who was creating that loud sound. Please stay here until I get some information about the sound," Damanak requested the lion and left.

Pingalak thought that it wasn't right for him to believe the jackal's words. Perhaps the jackal could be interested in befriending the enemy and dethroning him. Thus thinking, Pingalak decided to follow the jackal and hide at a safe distance in the forest and watch its movements. Pingalak accordingly went and hid in the forest.

In the meantime, Damanak also entered the forest and approached Sanjeevak. He was pleased to find that Sanjeevak was only a bull! Having learnt about the identity of the sound's source, Damanak thought: 'A king stricken with a crisis is always dependent on his ministers. Therefore, the ministers always pray and make sure that the king always remains in misery.'

Insight: Try to make yourself indispensable to your superiors by cultivating knowledge and abilities they don't possess; as long as these do not become obsolete, they will need you and keep consulting you.

Thinking thus, Damanak went to Pingalak, who sat in front of him suppressing his fear. Pingalak asked: "Have you seen the creature, Damanak?"

Damanak replied: "Yes, your majesty, I have seen him and possibly he might have also seen you. But strong and superior people don't inflict pain on the weaker and may be that was the reason he did not hurt you."

The gale does not uproot grass, which is tender and bends before the wind. Similarly, superior people equipped with high intelligence possess a humble nature. They show their bravery against stronger people.

Damanak said: "Your majesty, it is true that the creature is courageous as well as strong and that we are weak and feeble. But if the king wishes I could bring that creature to your service."

Pingalak breathed a sigh of relief and asked: "Is this really possible?"

Damanak replied: "Yes, it is possible to do anything with the help of intelligence. It has also been said: *'It is easier to win a war with the help of intelligence rather than trying to win it through physical might.'*"

Pingalak replied: "If it is so, I appoint you to the post of minister right now and bestow on you discretionary powers to punish and reward accordingly."

After this, Damanak approached Sanjeevak and frightened him with tales of the might of wild animals! He made friends with the bull and assured him that he would introduce him to Pingalak, the lion king. Damanak told Sanjeevak that it was in his best interests that he seek pardon from the king and earn his patronage. "Do not waste your strength whimsically. I will become the minister of the state and then we both shall enjoy the comforts and luxuries of the royal court," Damanak coaxed the bull. "*An egoistical person who does not respect everyone equally is degraded and suffers a fall in his position,* like Dantil, though he may be honoured by the king."

Sanjeevak asked Damanak: "How is that?"

Damanak narrated the story of Dantil to Sanjeevak.

Insight: From among the whole array of animals, jackals and foxes are chosen to portray the king's ministers. The author obviously wanted to convey that in reality too politicians are like jackals and foxes. Beware of their cunning. It would be wise not to take them at their face value. Damanak the jackal urged the bull to seek pardon from the king and to earn his patronage, with the lure of a bribe: "I will become the minister of the state and then we both shall enjoy the comforts and luxuries of the royal court." At the same time, he gave the king an impression that the bull was stronger than him and he himself was smart enough to appease the bull and win his friendship, thus ingratiating himself with the king. As politicians or leaders, we should control ourselves lest we too become unscrupulous and two-faced like Damanak. As for the common man, he should beware of unscrupulous politicians who can play double games to promote their vested interests.

The Story of Dantil

Long ago there was a city called Vardhaman where a rich businessman lived. His name was Dantil and he was the headman of the city. Dantil had pleased the king with his work. During his marriage, Dantil invited the king, the queens and the ministers and honoured them all. At that time, a sweeper named Gorambh arrived and occupied a higher seat. This was an insult to the king. Hence the sweeper was thrown out of Dantil's haveli.

Feeling terribly insulted, the sweeper could not sleep for many nights. Gorambh was smouldering for vengeance. He always kept on devising ways of how he could create a rift between the king and Dantil.

One day, early in the morning when the king was relaxing, Gorambh went near the window of the king's bedroom and said aloud: "It is surprising Dantil has become so bold that he goes and hugs the queen."

Listening to this, the king immediately woke up and asked Gorambh if his words were true. He asked: "Did Dantil really hug the queen?"

Gorambh replied: "Your Highness, I was playing a game of cards with my friend late last night and thereafter could not sleep. My friend frequently visits Dantil's home. He says he overheard Dantil saying: 'I have enjoyed closer contacts with the queen.' But I don't remember the exact words. I am feeling very sleepy now, so I don't know what I blabbered."

The king thought that the sweeper came here daily and Dantil was also a routine visitor. It could be possible that Gorambh might have seen the queen hugging Dantil. It is also said that the person who has latent desires during the day, utters them during his sleep. The latent emotions or feelings of a person are expressed while drinking or dreaming. That is why one should not believe women because they talk to one and look at another with desirous eyes and think about the third in their heart.

Fire is not satisfied with wood. Oceans are not satisfied with rivers. In the same way, women are not even satisfied with many men. Contemplating the character of women, the king felt sorry and passed a decree that Dantil should henceforth not be allowed to enter the court. This decree confused and surprised Dantil. He could not figure out the possible reason behind this unexpected development. He had not committed any crime that would make the king unhappy.

One day, Dantil tried to enter the court but was stopped by the guards. Seeing this, Gorambh laughed and said to the guards: "O guards, this man himself decides about the punishment or pardon. If you stop him, you shall be insulted in the same way that I was insulted by him."

Dantil heard this and thought that Gorambh might have said something to the king that resulted in his banishment. So Dantil invited the sweeper Gorambh home and gifted him articles and clothes. Expressing repentance for his misdeeds, Dantil begged his pardon. Gorambh forgave Dantil and assured him that the king would reappoint and invite him to the court.

The very next day in the morning, Gorambh went outside the king's bedroom to sweep and mumbled near the window, "It is very surprising indeed that our king is like a fool who eats cucumber while answering nature's call."

The king overheard this and was annoyed. He asked angrily: "Why do you talk all this nonsense? You are a servant of this house, that is the reason why I forgive you."

Gorambh replied apologetically: "I gambled throughout the night. I'm feeling very sleepy right now. I don't know what I mumbled. Please forgive me. I was really not in my senses."

Suddenly, it struck the king that just as the sweeper said something absurd about him, he could have said something equally idiotic about Dantil, when he wasn't in his senses. It was sure that Dantil was a good man and had no illicit relations with the queen. So he needs to be reinstated, the king thought.

He immediately summoned his ministers and asked them to invite Dantil to the court with honour and respect. When Dantil received this news he was happy.

Insight 1: Do not base your actions upon rumour or gossip. Make sure of your facts before taking a decision. Otherwise you are likely to reap unfavourable consequences and cause suffering to the people concerned and yourself.

Insight 2: Humiliating and insulting an underling for a mistake in his social demeanour is harsh treatment and not worthy of a leader. Such a leader could also have to face grave consequences as the subordinate will probably be bent upon revenge and see that the one who caused him humiliation ends up with loss of favour from those at the top.

Listening to all this, Sanjeevak said, "O Lord, I will do whatever you expect from me. Please take me to Pingalak."

Damanak escorted Sanjeevak to Pingalak and introduced him to the king. Very soon, the bull and the lion became fast friends. In the company of Sanjeevak and listening to his tales, Pingalak gave up violence and killing of animals. Pingalak now began to like Sanjeevak so much that he wouldn't even pay attention to Damanak when Sanjeevak accompanied him.

As a result, all the carnivorous animals that lived on meat began to starve. Moreover, Damanak's family left him and went away. Seeing this, Damanak was very unhappy. Karkat blamed Damanak for the situation. It was because of Damanak that the bull met the lion and transformed him into a herbivore as a result of which they were now starving.

Damanak accepted blame for his folly and said: "Pingalak has given up hunting and eating meat. Our families are starving. We will have to change the king's lifestyle. Although the king has been misguided, it is our duty as his ministers to bring him on the right path. Yes, it is not the king's mistake but mine. *We have lost our honour by our misdeeds.*"

Insight: The jackals realised that their selfish motives had landed them in trouble.

Damanak then narrated the following tale to Karkat.

The Story of Kaulik and the Princess

Two friends lived in a city. One was a weaver and the other a carpenter.

Once a festival was organised in the city. People from far-off places thronged the festival. The two friends also went to the festival, where they saw a princess riding an elephant escorted by eunuchs. The weaver was so infatuated by the irresistible beauty of the princess that he fell in love with her at once and swooned. His friend carried him home and called a doctor. When the weaver came around, he informed the carpenter that unless the princess embraced him, he would die. He said: "O friend! Let me die as I know that I won't be able to marry her, no matter how hard I try."

The carpenter consoled his friend: "Rest assured and have patience. You will certainly get the princess."

This reply puzzled the weaver. He asked how it could be possible.

Then his friend carved a Garuda out of shorea (sal) wood. He also carved two arms, a conch, a lotus, a wheel and a mace with the same wood and gave it to the weaver. The carpenter also taught him how to fly the Garuda.

The weaver then took on the guise of Lord Vishnu, rode the Garuda and flew towards the palace where the princess lived. When he reached the palace he found her sleeping. He said: "O princess! Are you sleeping or awake? I have come to meet you leaving behind Lakshmi at Ksheersagar. I want to marry you, so please accept me as your husband."

The princess was amazed at the appearance of Lord Vishnu. She awakened from her sleep and said: "How can we have a relationship? I am a human being, whereas you are the Lord of all the three worlds."

The weaver then convinced her that she was in reality Radha — who was born in Gokul. "You are the same Radha, my wife, and you have been born as a princess in this birth, and this is the reason why I came here," he said.

The princess advised him to take her father's permission. The weaver did not want to meet her father. He began to make excuses:

"I am invisible. Mortals cannot see me. What conversation can I have with your father? Do as I say, otherwise I will curse your father and your entire clan to destruction."

The weaver then held the terrified princess by the hand, forcibly took her on the bed and satisfied his lust. He returned back home early in the morning.

This continued for many nights. The weaver was happy that he was able to satisfy his lust uninterruptedly.

The eunuchs who were guarding the princess were amazed to notice significant changes in her. They suspected that the virginity of the princess was no longer intact. They wondered: "How did this happen? Who is the man responsible for destroying her virginity? Above all, how did he manage to sneak through such foolproof security?"

They decided to inform the king about the entire development. When the king heard about the changes in his daughter, he became very sad and worried. He consulted the queen and advised her to find out the truth behind the allegation. The queen went to the princess and was very angry when she discovered scratches and other marks on her body acquired during love play. When the princess narrated the whole story, the queen felt very pleased that her daughter had the good fortune of making love to Lord Vishnu. The queen went back to the king and said: "You have become the father-in-law of Lord Vishnu. Our daughter has tied the nuptial knot with Him. If you don't believe me, you can see Him tonight."

The king too felt very happy and began considering himself very fortunate. He said: "O queen! We are blessed that Lord Vishnu has become our son-in-law. Now I will vanquish all the other kings with the blessings of Lord Vishnu."

Now the king eagerly awaited the arrival of night, so that he could see his son-in-law. When night came, the king and queen peeped through the window. Both were convinced when they saw Kaulik the weaver disguised as Lord Vishnu.

Since then onwards, the king began to develop enmity with the neighbouring states. He was certain that since 'Lord Vishnu' was on his side, nobody would be able to fight him. He also asked his daughter to make a request to Lord Vishnu in this regard.

Very soon, enemies attacked his kingdom from all sides and in no time defeated the king. His daughter appealed to 'Lord Vishnu' to save her father. But Kaulik only gave hollow assurances.

At last, when the king was left with only one fort in his possession, Kaulik the weaver was forced to come to his help. He feared that if the king lost even this last fort, everybody's faith in him would vanish and he would no longer be able to meet the princess.

The weaver decided to make his appearance at an appropriate elevation in the sky. He mounted on the back of his wooden Garuda with all his weapons. 'Perhaps the enemies will get frightened on seeing me,' he thought.

Narrating the story, Damanak paused and continued: "This way, Kaulik mounted his wooden Garuda and flew up in the sky to fight beside the king."

Now, watching from the heavens above, Lord Vishnu told Garuda, "O Garuda! This Kaulik has invited his death. We must save his life otherwise people will no longer have faith in me. If he is killed, people will think that I have been killed. People will stop worshipping me."

Lord Vishnu then instructed Garuda to merge his divine form into the wooden Garuda. And Lord Vishnu Himself entered Kaulik's body.

After the battle was over, the victorious Kaulik descended to the earth. Kaulik introduced himself to the king and revealed his real identity. In his extreme happiness, the victorious king had his daughter married to Kaulik and bequeathed his kingdom to him.

After narrating the story, Damanak said: *"An enterprising man can achieve anything and nothing is beyond his reach."*

Insight: Unremitting enterprise and persistence can accomplish much that great intelligence sometimes cannot achieve. Be prepared for hard work to achieve your goals. One who loses his fear of hard work is capable of winning almost anything he desires. On the other hand if, like the king, you allow your highly-placed contacts to make you overconfident and proud, this will create ill will and show you in poor public light and thus you could lose your standing and power.

Karkat agreed but still doubted Damanak's intelligence to cause differences between Sanjeevak and Pingalak. But Damanak was confident of his ability. He said: *"The task which can be accomplished just by applying clever means cannot be accomplished by being valiant.* Just as the crow killed a black cobra with the help of a golden chain."

Karkat requested Damanak to tell him this tale.

The Crows and the Cobra

Once upon a time, a father-crow, mother-crow and their young ones lived on a tree. Under the tree a cobra lived in its hole. One day the cobra crawled up the tree and ate the young crows. The mother-crow told the father-crow: "Let us fly away from this tree; to-morrow the serpent may come and eat us."

But the father-crow replied: "Do not be afraid dear; do as I tell you. The prince will come here to-morrow to bathe in the river. Then he will leave his necklace on the bank. When he bathes, take hold of the necklace and put it into the serpent's hole."

The mother-crow did as she was told. The servants saw the mother-crow stealing the necklace and followed it; but the mother-crow threw the necklace into the serpent's hole. The servants dug up the hole, killed the serpent and took hold of the necklace.

Thereafter, the father-crow and mother-crow lived happily on the same tree.

Insight: Find creative ways to solve your problems rather than running away from them. Do not underestimate the importance of certain things in life. Ignoring the strong maternal instinct of protectiveness towards the young, or ignorance of such an instinct, cost the cobra its life.

Damanak mentioned how a greedy crane used to devour all types of fish in a pond. Because of its excessive greed, the crane was ultimately killed by a crab.

Karkat asked: "How did the crab kill the crane?"

Damanak then narrated the following story:

27

The Crane and the Crab

In a forest, there was a lake. Many animals used to gather around the lake to drink water from it. A crane too lived there but because of old age was unable to catch its prey.

Once the crane was very hungry. Standing at the bank of the lake, it was weeping. Seeing him weep, a crab asked why he was weeping. The crane deceitfully replied: "Son, I have embraced asceticism to atone for my sins which I acquired by devouring fish from this lake. Now I have taken a vow to end my life by observing a fast unto death. This is the reason why I do not hunt fish even when I have an opportunity."

The crab asked him: "But why are you weeping?"

The crane replied that he was attached to the lake and all the creatures living in it. "I have grown up near this lake. I have played with the creatures living in this lake. But I have come to know from astrologers that it will not rain for the next 12 years. If this really happens, the lake will dry up. This thought makes me weep because I cannot bear to see others in pain. So I have decided to end my life."

When the fish saw the crane narrating a story to the crab, they all swarmed to the bank. When they learnt about the astrologer's forecast, fear gripped them all. They asked the crane if there was any way to escape this inevitable danger.

The crane said: "At a little distance from this lake, there is a very big reservoir which has so much water that it will not dry up even if it does not rain for 24 years. All the creatures from the surrounding lakes are making their way to the reservoir. You all too must go to the reservoir."

Hearing this, the fish expressed their inability to reach the reservoir: "How can we reach the reservoir when we cannot walk?"

The crane then assured them of help. He said: "I will carry all of you on my back one by one to the reservoir."

The crane then carried a fish on his back to an isolated place and perching on a rock smashed it to death before eating it. One by one, the crane cunningly took the fish from the lake and had its fill. This continued for many days.

One day the crab said to the crane: "How cruel of you! I was the first to take up this serious matter with you, but until now you have not paid any attention to me. Today, you should help me reach the reservoir."

The crane was fed up with the monotonous taste of fish, so when he heard the crab's desire, he was happy. He felt it would be a nice change of diet. He therefore carried the crab on his back and flew towards the rock. When the crab saw bones of the fish scattered all around the rock, he grew suspicious, but did not show his fear and asked: "How far is the reservoir from here?"

At this the crane replied: "Do you see that rock? This is the reservoir! Now you too will meet the same fate as the fish."

As soon as the crane perched on the rock, the crab caught hold of the crane's neck and strangled it to death.

Insight: Do not take people's promises at their face value. Deceitful people abound who are ready to take advantage of the unwary. Beware of them. They use different tactics, including creating fear and panic, like the crane did. Also, as was the case with the crane, excessive greed and extreme cunning can be counterproductive. Sooner or later such an individual will find someone even more cunning than himself and, maybe, even more vengeful than he could have imagined... There are more effective ways of surviving and prospering than by swindling others, which may even cost one one's life.

Completing his story, Damanak said: *"Only an intelligent man has strength, whereas a stupid but muscular person is weak.* For this reason, a lion, which was very proud of its strength, was killed by a small hare."

Karkat curiously asked: "How did this happen?"

The Lion and the Hare

A lion named Bhasurak lived in a forest. Daily it would kill many animals without any reason. All the animals were extremely scared of the lion.

So they devised a plan to save their lives and accordingly approached the lion and said: "Every day, you unnecessarily kill numerous animals. One animal a day is enough to satisfy your hunger. If the killings continue like this, the forest will soon be devoid of animals. So we have decided that everyday one of us will voluntarily come to you to be your food. This way you will be able to have your food without making any effort."

Bhasurak agreed, but warned them: "The day an animal fails to reach me, I will kill all of you."

Since that day, one animal went to the lion every day. The lion would kill and devour the animal.

One day it was the turn of a small hare. The thought of imminent death had frightened him. The hare proceeded towards the lion, as he had no choice. He walked very slowly with heavy feet.

On the way, he saw a well. He peeped into it and saw his reflection in the water. An idea flashed into his mind. He made a plan to meet the lion very late in the evening. When Bhasurak saw the hare, he asked furiously: "Why are you so late?"

According to his plan, the hare narrated a concocted story: "Lord! Since I am a very small animal, I thought that only eating me would not satisfy your hunger. Hence four other hares had also accompanied me. We were feeling proud that at last in our lives we would be able to serve you. But on the way, we met another lion who said that he was the king of this forest. When we told him that we were getting late, as we had to reach you, he began abusing you. After repeated requests, he allowed me to come here with the instruction that you must accept his supremacy."

Bhasurak's anger knew no bounds. He said: "Tell me, where does he live?"

The hare took him right up to the well and told him that the challenger lived in it. When the lion peeped into the well, he saw his own reflection in the water. Mistaking it for another lion, Bhasurak let out a loud roar. The roar echoed back from the well. Bhasurak thought that the challenger was roaring in reply to his roar. By now, Bhasurak's temper had shot high and the next moment he jumped into the well. He never returned.

Insight: Intelligence is more fruitful than brute force in accomplishing anything. Try to find creative solutions to your problems. You will find the solutions more satisfying than trying to solve them the routine way. The message for the modern leader is that brains have an upper hand over brawn; so spend more time in developing your mental abilities than exercising in the gym.

Damanak continued: "If you permit me, I can create friction between Pingalak and Sanjeevak."

Karkat permitted him to go, wishing him good luck.

Damanak then reached the place where Pingalak was staying. Sanjeevak didn't happen to be around. Greeting Pingalak, Damanak sat beside him quietly. Pingalak asked him where he had been all these days. Damanak said: "Sir, I did not meet you all these days as there was no specific purpose, but the prospect of you losing your kingdom has forced me to come here again."

Pingalak could not understand what exactly Damanak meant. He asked Damanak to elaborate his point.

Damanak said: "Lord! Sanjeevak is jealous of you. He has revealed to me his plan to kill you. He wants to become the king. He has also offered me the post of a minister."

Pingalak was disturbed to know all this, but did not completely believe Damanak's words. Damanak then convinced him with more deceitful statements, but Pingalak said: "Even if Sanjeevak maintains enmity towards me, I won't stoop to his level."

Finding Pingalak somewhat influenced by his words, Damanak continued: "Forgiving an enemy is not a sound policy. Moreover, you are not a vegetarian. How then can you have a long-lasting friendship with a vegetarian? Sanjeevak has not only destroyed your qualities but also deviated you from your path. Your conduct should be in the same manner as that of water. A drop of water that falls on a hot iron evaporates but the same water looks as beautiful as a pearl if it falls on the leaf of a lotus or on a blade of grass. The same water is converted into a pearl if it falls into a shell during the constellation Swati. Therefore, it has been rightly said that *a person is known by the company he keeps*. It is also said *that one must never give refuge to a person whose nature is unknown*. A louse did so and was killed because of the fault of a tick."

Pingalak curiously asked: "How did this happen?"

Damanak narrated the story of the tick and the louse:

Insight: The above story is a classic example of causing enmity and rift between friends by maligning one friend to another. It is also an example of twisting a wise statement and misusing it to influence someone: 'Forgiving the enemy is not a sound policy,' the jackal tells the lion. Foxy as this bit of advice is, it overlooks the precaution that should have been taken to express the following: if an enemy is not repentant for the harm he has caused you, he is still your enemy and forgiving such a person is not a good policy.

Observation: Damanak proves to be an expert in deceitfulness. He has no qualms about mixing sound advice and philosophy with his lies to create trouble in order to spoil the great friendship between Sanjeevak and Pingalak for his personal advantage. Beware of the Damanaks around you! They can ruin not only your career but also your life.

The Bedbug and the Louse

A louse named Mandavisarpini lived in a bedsheet on the king's bed. She would pass her days happily sucking the king's blood.

One day a tick named Agnimukh arrived in the king's bedroom. Mandavisarpini sadly asked: "From where have you arrived to live in a place which is fit only for me? Go back soon before anybody sees you."

The tick requested the louse: "It is improper to turn back even a wicked person who has arrived at your home as a guest. It is the duty of a householder to treat a guest well; it helps him attain heaven.

"Besides, I have tasted the blood of men from all strata except a king's. The blood of common people tastes sour, sharp or bitter. I know that the blood of a king must be sweet in taste. If you allow me to taste the sweet blood of the king, I will be highly obliged. Moreover, all such activities are performed only for the sake of satisfying one's hunger. Your guest desires food from you. It is not good on your part to taste the king's sweet blood all alone."

Mandavisarpini the louse agreed, but warned the tick: "You mean tick! I suck the king's blood only when he is fast asleep. You too must do the same."

Agnimukh agreed. In the meantime, the king arrived and lay down on the bed. The impatient tick wanted to taste the king's blood in a hurry. He could not even wait for the king to fall asleep and began to bite him while he was still awake.

Bitten by the tick, the king got up in pain. He called his attendants and instructed them to find out whether it was a tick or a louse that had bitten him. As the search began, the tricky tick hurriedly hid between the crevices of the bedstead, but the poor, sluggish louse was caught while she was trying to hide within the folds of the bedsheet. The king's attendants killed her at once.

Insight: Don't be fooled by glib talk motivated by self-interest if that interest does not coincide with yours. Otherwise your interests are likely to be sacrificed if you follow such glib advice. Harbouring employees or guests of an unknown origin or character may have dangerous consequences.

After narrating the tale, Damanak told Pingalak: "Lord, it would be better if Sanjeevak were kept at a distance because it is said that a person who develops intimacy with an outsider, after abandoning his close friends and relatives, meets certain death. Just as a king, Kakuddroom, was killed."

Curious to know about the story of King Kakuddroom, Pingalak asked: "How did that happen?"

Damanak then narrated the following story...

King Kakuddroom, the Jackal

A jackal named Chandarav used to live in a forest. Once, feeling restless due to hunger, he strayed into the city. When some dogs saw him, they began to chase him, barking furiously. To save his life, the jackal entered the home of a dyer and fell into an earthen trough in which a solution of indigo was stored.

When the dogs went away, the jackal came out of the trough. Now he was not the same jackal; his colour had changed to blue!

The jackal proceeded towards the forest. All the animals were terrified on seeing such a strange animal. They started running helter-skelter. The jackal was very pleased to see this. He shouted: "Listen! Lord Brahma has sent me to rule over you, because this forest does not have any king. From today, I am your king. I assure you that I will rule justly. So do not be afraid of me. My name is Kakuddroom."

All the animals came and gathered around him. They requested the jackal to accept their services. The jackal appointed the lion as his minister. Similarly the tiger, the leopard and the fox were entrusted with various jobs. But he drove the other jackals out of the forest.

In this way, the jackal enjoyed ruling. All the animals, including the lion, were at his service now. One day, the exiled jackals started howling in groups.

Kakuddroom too heard their howling. He could not control himself and began howling along with them. When the lion and other animals heard him howl, they discovered his real identity — he was just an ordinary jackal! They were ashamed that the jackal had fooled them for so long. They at once killed the pretender.

One who abandons his kith and kin is killed just like the jackal.

Insight: To maintain your pretence you need an unfailing memory. Otherwise you are likely to be discovered sooner or later and made a fool of and your reputation destroyed. It is impossible to live in a make-believe world where you are acting a role all the time. As soon as you feel comfortable in this role and let your guard down, you will certainly show your true colours and let everyone see what is below the gold plating or the indigo!

After completing his story, and feeling assured that Pingalak had fallen into his trap, Damanak went to meet Sanjeevak.

He made salutations to Sanjeevak and sat quietly with a gloomy face. When Sanjeevak saw his worried face, he asked if there was any problem.

Damanak replied: "How can anybody be well with a servant because the person who is a servant of royalty has his wealth controlled by others; not only is he restless, he is also unsure about the safety of his life."

Sanjeevak could not understand anything and said: "What are you trying to say? Say it clearly."

Realising that the iron was hot, Damanak said: "Pingalak harbours ill intentions towards you. He was saying he would kill you the next morning. I tried to dissuade him but he said that the enmity between him and you was natural because he is a carnivore and you are a herbivore. When I found him unrelenting, I decided to inform you."

Sanjeevak was so shocked by his words that he fainted! When he regained consciousness, he told Damanak: "It was my mistake to have befriended Pingalak. Even if I try to make him understand my point, he won't understand it. I know the reason behind his anger. Being jealous of the favour shown by my master, somebody has poisoned Pingalak's mind. Learned people perform their tasks without caring for the means they apply. It doesn't matter to them whether the means are just or unjust, just as the crow and other animals did with the camel."

Damanak curiously asked: "Where and how did that happen?"

Sanjeevak then narrated the following tale:

Kathanak, the Camel

Once there lived a lion in a forest. His name was Madotkar. A crow, a leopard and a jackal were his followers. Once he saw a camel that had strayed into the forest. The name of the camel was Kathanak. When the lion saw the camel, he was amazed because he had never seen a camel in his life.

He said: "Look at him! Just find out if he is a wild animal or if he belongs to a village."

The crow said: "That animal belongs to a village. It is a camel and is worth eating, so you must kill him."

But the lion refused to kill the camel. He said: "It will be improper on my part to kill this camel because he has come to my place and so he is my guest."

The lion then instructed the crow, leopard and jackal to fetch the camel with full honour, saying he would like to know why it had strayed into the forest. When the camel arrived, the lion asked him why he had come into the forest. The camel replied that he had escaped from his home because his master tortured him.

The lion felt sorry for him. He asked the camel to live in the forest without fear. Since then, the camel began living in the forest.

Once the lion had a fight with an elephant and was badly injured by its tusks. Now he was unable to hunt. Even the crow, leopard and jackal began to starve because they used to eat the leftovers of the animals killed by the lion.

The lion felt pity because of their condition. He instructed them to find such an animal, which he could kill even in his injured condition.

The crow and the jackal wandered all around the forest but could not find such an animal. At last, both of them thought of killing the camel.

"But our master has granted him protection. How can we dare kill him?" the crow wondered.

Then both of them went to the lion to seek his permission to kill the camel. "We did not find any animal. We are dying of hunger. Your condition seems to be the same. With your permission, can we kill Kathanak and satisfy our hunger?" asked the jackal.

At this, the lion was very angry. "Shame on you! Don't you know that I have granted him protection? I will kill you the moment you mention this another time. I do not want to commit a sin by killing my guest," said the lion.

The jackal then said: "Lord, you would certainly commit a sin if you kill him. You will, however, not commit any sin if Kathanak is ready to sacrifice his life voluntarily to protect your life from hunger. If this is not possible, you can kill any of us to satisfy your hunger, because if you die of starvation, we too will have to face the same consequence sooner or later."

Madotkar the lion said, "Do as you like."

Now according to his plan, the jackal said to his friends assembled there: "Look, the condition of our master has deteriorated. At this rate, he will soon starve to death. If this happens, who will protect us? Let us make a sacrifice to save him so that he survives and we too are free from our indebtedness towards him."

37

Saying this, the jackal sat down before the lion with tears in his eyes. The crow was very impressed by the jackal's love for his master. He did not want to remain behind. He said: "Lord! Save your life by devouring me, so that I can attain salvation."

The jackal then said: "How can the master be satisfied by devouring you. You are so small. Moreover, the Scriptures say that eating the flesh of a crow leads to grave sin. By expressing your feelings, you have already freed yourself from your indebtedness towards him. Now, move aside. Lord, save your life by eating me so that I can attain both the worlds."

Listening to all this, the leopard said: "Lord! Devour me so that I can attain salvation."

Unaware of the jackal's plan, Kathanak fell into the trap. Since the lion did not kill anybody, though everybody was most willing to die, *he too decided to please the lion with flattering words.* He said: "O leopard! How can the master kill you? You belong to the same family of carnivores. Move aside and let me request the master."

Then turning towards the lion, the camel said: "Lord! All these animals are not fit to be your food. Save your life by killing me so that I can attain both the worlds."

Hardly had Kathanak finished speaking, when the lion gestured to the other animals. Immediately, the tiger, leopard and jackal tore the camel's stomach apart, killing him.

Insight 1: It is important to know whom to trust and whom not to trust. Following untrustworthy advice can be your undoing. Always stay alert and on the lookout for self-centred people ready to outmanoeuvre you. On your part, while sincerity can take you a long way in life, flattery will not take you too far – it brought about the camel's end.

Insight 2: If you think of yourself as a victim all the time, you are likely to attract those who will ultimately turn you into one.

Insight 3: Do not assume that those you associate with are your allies till you have double-checked and they have proved themselves.

After finishing this story, Sanjeevak said: "I will not shift to another place even if my master is angry with me, because people who have power also have long reach. They can catch their enemies, no matter where they go. So I have no option except to battle him."

When Damanak heard this, he was worried that if Sanjeevak inflicted injuries on Pingalak with his sharp horns, it would be unfortunate. Damanak wanted to avoid the fight. Damanak said: "Friend! What is the use of a fight between master and servant? One should protect oneself when faced with a powerful enemy, otherwise he is bound to meet the fate of the lapwing who in his arrogance was destroyed by the sea."

Sanjeevak asked him to narrate the story of the lapwing and the sea.

The Lapwing and the Sea

A lapwing lived with his wife near the sea. His wife's pregnancy period was about to mature. She requested her husband to find a safe place to lay the eggs.

The lapwing instructed her to lay her eggs on the seashore. But his wife was uncertain. She said: "The seashore is not a safe place, because high tides occur on the full moon day in which even a big elephant could be submerged. So look out for some other place which is safe."

The lapwing laughed loudly. He then said arrogantly: "The sea is not capable of destroying my offspring. Who would try to enter fire deliberately? Who would try to wake up a sleeping lion? Who would challenge the lord of death? So lay your eggs without fear."

The sea was listening to the arrogant words of the lapwing and decided to teach him a lesson.

After laying her eggs, the mother lapwing went to fetch some grains. Finding the time opportune, the sea drowned the eggs with a wave. When the mother lapwing did not find her eggs after her return, she felt very sad.

She said: "I had warned you about this and today my words have come true. Somebody has rightly said that a person who does not listen to his friends' advice is destroyed like the tortoise."

Insight: It is unwise to ignore well-meant friendly advice out of arrogance. It is important to listen to advice from all quarters and then act on the best evidence available. Have arrogance and false pride ever given anyone any returns? Do they serve any positive purpose at all? When we come across arrogance personified, do we feel any liking or respect for that person? Or do these attributes make the person the butt of ridicule? These questions will help you decide if you need to free yourself from any trace of arrogance.

The lapwing asked curiously: "How was the tortoise destroyed?"

Then his wife narrated the following story:

The Swans and the Tortoise

A tortoise named Kumbagreeva once lived in a lake. Two swans, which were his friends, also lived in the same lake. Their names were Sankat and Vikat.

Both swans would tell the tortoise stories about sages. Once it did not rain for many months. The level of the water in the lake also began falling. The swans were worried about the tortoise and asked him: "Friend! Now only the mud remains in the lake. How will you survive?"

Kumbagreeva replied: "I am worried too. But let us patiently think about a way to get rid of this problem."

The tortoise then revealed his plan to both swans: "Bring a rope or a wooden stick. The two of you fly holding both the ends in your beaks. I will hold the rope or stick in the middle. This way both of you can carry me to a lake full of water."

The swans agreed but they warned him against opening his mouth, otherwise he would fall down to earth.

The tortoise nodded. The swans carried the tortoise according to the plan. As they were flying over a city, people down below saw the amazing scene. They started shouting: "Look at this! How amazing!"

When the tortoise heard this noise, he became curious. He asked: "What is this fuss about?"

But as soon as the tortoise opened his mouth, he fell down to the earth. The people caught and killed him.

Insight 1: Beware of impulsive talk and action. They can have fatal consequences. It may then be too late to take remedial measures.

Insight 2: You can achieve your aims if you concentrate on the task at hand. Idle banter can distract you from what is important in life – indulge in it and see the opportunities pass you by. In the case of the tortoise, prattle led to the loss of its life.

After finishing her story the mother lapwing said: *"A person who performs his actions, keeping the future in mind and one who tries to find a solution to his problems, achieves happiness even when faced with calamity. On the other hand, one who leaves himself to his destiny gets destroyed."*

The lapwing curiously asked: "How does one who leaves himself to his destiny get destroyed?"

His wife then narrated the following story:

The Story of the Three Fish

In a lake there once lived three fish. Their names were Anagatvidhata, Pratyutpannamati and Yabhdavishya. One day, some fishermen passed by the lake. They were very pleased to see the lake full of fish. They decided to fish in the lake the next day.

When Anagatvidhata heard about their plan, she told her friends: "Did you hear that? We must go to some other lake in the night, because it is said that one should flee when faced with a powerful enemy."

Pratyutpannamati agreed with her, but Yabhdavishya said: "Your decision is not proper. Why should we abandon this lake, which belonged to our forefathers? If we really are destined to die, then we will die, no matter where we go. I will remain here. Both of you are free to make your decision."

In this situation, Anagavidhata and Pratyutpannamati left that lake for some other lake.

The fishermen came in the morning and caught Yabhdavishya in their net along with some other fish.

Insight 1: Tradition does not always ensure safety. When new problems arise, look out for new solutions, perhaps in new environments if the old environment has become risky. At times we have to be prepared to break away from our roots to safeguard our lives; that does not mean our roots are unimportant, but that our inability to be flexible and let go can become not only self-destructive but senseless and irresponsible. It can also reveal a block against balancing the utopian and the real world in which we live – an unwillingness to be realistic and face reality boldly.

Insight 2: Any action taken when the enemy or tragedy strikes is a valiant effort. Taking things lying down in adversity is deplorable. If it is in your hands to control your destiny, it is foolish to stay put and not take any action – it may be a God-sent opportunity that you are throwing to the winds and foolishly allowing inimical forces to destroy you.

After he heard the story, the lapwing said to his wife: "Do you think I am like Yabhdavishya? You just wait and see how I dry up the sea with my beak."

At this his wife said: "There is no comparison between you and the sea because *the anger of an incapable man destroys only him.* Moreover, a person who faces his mighty enemy without realising his capability is destroyed like an insect trapped inside a flame."

The lapwing told his wife not to underestimate his power and strength, saying: "Dear! *What one needs is enthusiasm and capability — it doesn't matter whether one is big or small. A big elephant is controlled by a small iron-hook. As soon as a small lamp starts burning, the great darkness disappears.*"

When the lapwing's wife saw that he was hell-bent on fighting the sea, she advised him to seek help from his friends, because *"even weak people become invincible in a group".*

She continued: "If you take your friends' assistance, you could probably fight against the sea in the same manner that a team comprising a woodpecker, sparrow, frog and fly destroyed a mighty elephant."

The lapwing wanted to hear the tale. His wife narrated the following story:

The Sparrow and the Elephant

There once lived a pair of sparrows in a forest. They had a nest on a big tree. The mother sparrow once laid eggs. One day an elephant came under the shade of the tree to take rest. It was very hot that day. The elephant playfully broke a particular branch on which the nest and the sparrows were resting. The eggs fell down and were smashed. The pair of sparrows survived somehow.

The female sparrow started wailing on seeing her eggs destroyed. Right then, a woodpecker by the name of Sudansunak arrived there. He was a friend of the sparrows. The woodpecker said: *"It's no use crying over a lost thing; a person who has died and time that has passed by never return."*

The mother sparrow said: "Whatever you say is absolutely right. But my sorrow will remain as long as that wicked elephant is alive. If you can help me in killing that mean elephant, only then will my sorrow be eliminated."

The woodpecker agreed to help the sparrows. He then went to call his friend Vinarwa, the fly. He narrated the whole story to her. The fly readily agreed to help the sparrows. Then she and the woodpecker went to Meghanand, the frog, who was a friend of the fly.

When the frog heard the whole story, he was very angry with the wicked elephant. He said: "What is this mean elephant before our collective strength?"

Then the frog devised a plan according to which the fly was to make a buzzing sound in the ears of the elephant, which would close his eyes in joy anticipating more. Right then, the woodpecker would blind him in both eyes with his pointed beak. In the afternoon, the blind elephant would be thirsty and search for water. Meghanand would then croak near a ravine. The elephant would follow his voice and walk towards the ravine, fall into it and die.

The plan worked successfully and the elephant died after falling into the ravine.

Insight 1: Teamwork can achieve wonders incapable of being achieved by individuals working alone. Although a hackneyed saying goes: 'Too many cooks spoil the broth', the saying does not apply when the action is well planned and each one has a role to play in order to achieve the desired result.

Insight 2: Even those who are big and powerful cannot afford to carelessly trample over the lives of small powerless people, in their own interest, or it will definitely backfire. The same applies to a leader.

The male lapwing said that he would follow her instructions. He went to call the peacock, the crane and the duck. He sought their help in drying up the sea. But understanding the impossible nature of the task, all of them refused. They told the lapwing that Garuda was their master. He could certainly help him in this regard.

All of them went to Garuda. They narrated the woes of the lapwing and requested Garuda to help him.

Garuda agreed to help the lapwing. He was thinking about a plan when suddenly a messenger of the Lord arrived. He informed Garuda about Lord Vishnu's desire of going to Amravati.

Garuda arrogantly said: "Go and tell Lord Vishnu to look for some other vehicle as I am going to dry up the sea."

The messenger was amazed. He had never seen Garuda in such an intemperate mood. He asked the reason for his anger. Garuda narrated how the sea had destroyed the eggs laid by the mother lapwing.

The messenger went back to Lord Vishnu and related the whole story. Lord Vishnu said that Garuda had every right to be angry with the sea. Lord Vishnu then went to pacify Garuda.

When Garuda saw Lord Vishnu, he was ashamed that because of him Lord Vishnu had to come on foot. But he was still angry with the sea. Garuda said: "Lord! The sea has dishonoured me by pilfering the eggs of my follower. I would have dried up the ocean by now, had you not arrived."

Empathising with the just anger of Garuda, Lord Vishnu drew out his feared Agnibaan to dry up the sea. The sea was terrified and returned the eggs to the lapwing. The lapwing then took the eggs to his wife.

Insight 1: Gauge your competitor's strength carefully and accurately before trying to overcome it. Otherwise, defeat could be costly for you and you could be humbled and embarrassed by the enemy.

Insight 2: In spite of Garuda's arrogance and misplaced anger at Lord Vishnu, it was finally Lord Vishnu himself who got the sea to behave, out of fear of his Agnibaan. Instead of showing off, whenever we have to do some important work that we would be unable to execute, it would be to our advantage to be humble enough to seek assistance from those more capable than us to accomplish the task.

After narrating this story, Damanak said: *"One should attack his enemy only after anticipating his strength and weakness correctly. One must also never stop in making one's best efforts."*

Sanjeevak remain unconvinced. He said: "Friend! I don't understand how Pingalak can harbour hatred towards me. I have always seen only his love for me, nothing else."

Damanak told him that it was not that difficult to find out. He said: "If his eyes become red after seeing you and his eyebrows are twisted and he starts licking the sides of his lips with his tongue, then you should understand that he is angry with you and harbours hatred towards you."

Damanak then warned Sanjeevak that Pingalak must not come to know about their secret talk at any cost. He also advised Sanjeevak to leave the place before nightfall.

Damanak then went to meet Karkat. He narrated the whole story of how he had planted the seed of suspicion between Pingalak and Sanjeevak. Damanak was confident that the next morning both of them would no longer remain friends.

Karkat was not at all pleased with Damanak's efforts in causing differences between the two of them. Damanak reminded him that one who does not destroy his enemies in the beginning pays the price of being destroyed by them ultimately. Damanak also said that *he had done all this just to acquire his ministership.*

Observation: *This is a classic example of using an innocent third party to satisfy your lust for power without any scruples about the safety and welfare of your victim. How common is this amongst leaders of our time? Do our leaders need the writings of an author from an ancient era to highlight the immensity of their moral degradation? Do they see themselves as worthy of their position? It is for them to ponder over these issues and for their followers to be wary...*

Continuing with his complaints against Sanjeevak, Damanak said: "Sanjeevak is my enemy because he has snatched my right from me. It was I who brought him to Pingalak, but he stabbed me in the back by sowing the seeds of doubt in the mind of Pingalak regarding my capabilities and became a minister himself, which is my right. *Those who are experts in politics accomplish their tasks even at the cost of others' pain and sorrow.*"

Observation: *Damanak is so blinded by his lust for power, he does not realise his philosophical observations (highlighted above) condemn himself first.*

"Fools are unable even to feed themselves regularly, as was the case with Chaturak — the jackal," Damanak concluded.

Karkat was very curious to know the tale of Chaturak. Damanak told him the following story:

Chaturak – the Jackal

A lion named Vajradanta lived in a forest. He had two attendants. One was Chaturak, the jackal and Kravyamukha, the wolf. Both the attendants followed their master wherever he went.

One day, the lion killed a female camel that had strayed from the rest of the herd and was pregnant. As soon as he tore apart her abdomen, he saw a calf inside. The lion, the jackal and the wolf devoured the camel, but took the infant camel to their den out of compassion. They named it Shankukarna. In due course of time, Shankukarna grew up.

One day, the lion had a fight with an elephant in which he was seriously injured. His injury rendered him incapable of hunting. The lion instructed the jackal and the wolf to search for such an animal, which he could kill even in his injured state. The jackal and the wolf tried hard but did not find such an animal.

So the jackal told Shankukarna: "Our master is unable to bear the pangs of hunger. If anything happens to him, it will be impossible for us to sustain our lives as easily as we do today."

Then the cunning jackal trapped the simpleton young camel with his glib talk, saying: "Give your body to the master at double-profit. This way, not only will his hunger be satisfied, your body will also double in size."

The young camel liked the idea. He too desired an enormous body like the other camels. He replied: "If this is so, then I will be glad to be of some help to the master. But I will do it only if witnessed by the lord of death."

Both of them went to the lion. Chaturak said: "Lord! We could not find any animal that you could kill even in your injured condition. Now the sun has already set. Shankukarna is willing to give his body, witnessed by the lord of death, at double-profit."

The lion agreed to this proposal. As soon as the lion nodded his permission, the jackal and the wolf killed Shankukarna. Vajradanta then went to have a bath, instructing both of them to take care of Shankukarna's body.

Now Chaturak wanted to devour the entire body himself. He thought of a plan to remove Kravyamukha from the way. Chaturak told Kravyamukha: "Friend! You seem to be very hungry! Eat this flesh! I will prove your innocence when the master returns."

As soon as Kravyamukha began to eat the flesh, Chaturak warned him that the master was coming. Kravyamukha moved aside. When the lion returned and saw that the heart of the camel was missing, he angrily asked: "Who has dared to touch this flesh?"

Kravyamukha looked at Chaturak in anticipation that he would defend him. Instead, Chaturak told Kravyamukha: "Why are you looking at my face? In spite of my repeated requests and warnings, you did not listen to me and began eating the flesh."

Kravyamukha fled from the scene.

As the lion was about to eat the body, he suddenly heard the sound of ringing bells. He sent Chaturak to find out where the sound was coming from. Chaturak went some distance and returned, saying: "Lord! Just run away if you can. The lord of death is angry with you, as you have killed Shankukarna prematurely. He is coming along with the ancestors of Shankukarna. One camel, which is ahead of all the other camels, has a bell hanging down his neck. That very bell is producing this fearful sound."

The lion went ahead to check for himself if this was true. When he saw a herd of camels approaching him, he was terrified and ran away. The jackal then happily devoured the entire body.

Insight 1: A careful strategy can overcome even the mighty. And if you combine it with the ability to use situations to your advantage at the opportune moment, it can result in a combination for success. That is how bright young people with new ideas succeed and prosper, while experienced companies, even when backed by money and reputation, fail. It would be commendable, however, if the new generation examined the nature of their strategies and tried to use just means to achieve their ends.

Insight 2: If you are gullible, there will be no dearth of people who will take advantage of your naiveté and figuratively eat you, like Shankukarna who was literally eaten. Therefore, thoroughly examine other people's proposals and, if necessary, seek expert advice before you agree to them, to avoid falling into fatal traps.

The story having been narrated, Damanak said: "This is the reason why I say that one must apply any means to accomplish a task."

After Damanak had gone, Sanjeevak thought that it was his mistake to have befriended Pingalak. "Where should I go? What should I do? Should I go back to Pingalak? Perhaps seeking his pardon will save my life."

So thinking, he went towards the place where Pingalak lived. When he reached there, he found Pingalak in the same posture as described by Damanak. This convinced Sanjeevak fully that whatever Damanak had said was absolutely right. He sat at a distance from Pingalak without greeting him. When Pingalak saw this, he too was convinced that Damanak was absolutely right in his inferences. Pingalak angrily pounced on Sanjeevak and injured his back. Sanjeevak in turn attacked him with his horns and somehow managed to keep at a distance.

When Karkat saw both of them injured, he admonished Damanak, saying he had not done the proper thing by causing a rift between them. Karkat said: "Damanak! You are a fool! If Pingalak dies from his injury, then all your efforts would go in vain and if he survives the attack, it would be inauspicious because the danger from an injured Sanjeevak will always loom large over him. So it is very essential for Sanjeevak to die. You fool! But actually, it is not your fault. *It is the fault of the master who was so naive to have such faith in you.* You are not fit to become his minister. Just as there is no use in making an effort to cut a stone with a knife, in the same way it is no use teaching an unworthy disciple, as was the case with Suchimukh."

Damanak wanted to hear the story of Suchimukh.

Karkat narrated the following story:

Suchimukh – the Bird

A t the foothills of a mountain, there once lived a troop of monkeys. One year, the winter was exceptionally chill due to excessive snowfall. As a result, the monkeys were unable to bear the cold.

A few monkeys saw some fibrous fruits on the ground, glowing like cinders. Mistaking them for cinders, they began blowing over them in order to make a fire. A bird named Suchimukh saw them doing this. She tried to convince them of the futility of their efforts but the monkeys did not listen to Suchimukh.

So Suchimukh retorted: "You all are fools! These are not cinders but fibrous fruits. You can never make fire with them. It would be better for you to look out for some shelter to protect yourselves from this chilling cold."

One of the monkeys angrily replied that it was none of her business, and they would do whatever they deemed fit. It has rightly been said that an intelligent person should not try to advise a person who fails repeatedly in accomplishing his task.

But Suchimukh repeatedly reminded them of the futility of their efforts. Already frustrated in their unsuccessful attempts at igniting a fire, the monkeys became angrier. They killed Suchimukh by dashing her against a rock.

Insight 1: Don't give unsolicited and unwanted advice. It can be interpreted as arrogance and will only create rancour. If you think you have valuable advice to provide, become a consultant and charge for your advice. Then, both you and your client will gain from your talent.

Insight 2: Voicing your opinion is different from forcing it on someone who is not even receptive. The monkeys were unable to bear the chilling cold and had already told Suchimukh, the bird, not to interfere because it was none of her business. Under these circumstances, it was foolish on the bird's part to insist on pushing her knowledge on those who were unable to benefit from it. In the event, she paid for this foolish behaviour with her life. The story is a warning for us not to interfere with things that are not our concern.

After completing the story, Karkat again admonished Damanak: "O fool, Damanak! In spite of my admonitions, you did not learn anything. As I said, it is not your fault, because knowledge is beneficial only for virtuous people, not for immoral people.

"A wicked person fails to realise his own impending destruction, being happy at the sorrows of other people. The torso keeps on dancing even after the head has been severed."

Then Karkat narrated the story of Dharmabuddhi and Paapbuddhi, which describes an incident where a man named Paapbuddhi was responsible for causing his father's death.

Dharmabuddhi and Paapbuddhi

Two friends used to live in a city. Their names were Dharmabuddhi and Paapbuddhi. Dharmabuddhi was very intelligent but Paapbuddhi lacked intelligence. One day, Paapbuddhi decided to migrate to another place and earn wealth with the help of Dharmabuddhi. He had also decided to ultimately misappropriate Dharmabuddhi's wealth deceitfully.

One day, Paapbuddhi told Dharmabuddhi: "Friend! Do you remember any of your deeds that would make you proud in your old age? Do you have anything worth remembering to share with your children? What would you tell your children unless you visit a foreign land? A person's life is meaningless unless he learns various languages and studies alien cultures by travelling to far-off places."

Dharmabuddhi got the point and agreed to accompany Paapbuddhi to a foreign land. One fine morning, both friends set out on their journey. They migrated to a foreign land and established their businesses. Both earned a lot of wealth and money. At last, they decided to return to their native place.

When they were about to reach their city, Paapbuddhi advised Dharmabuddhi: "Friend! It would not be proper for us to go to our houses with so much wealth. Our relatives and friends would begin demanding money from us. Therefore, we must bury a major portion of our wealth in the ground right here in this forest and carry as little money as we can. We will come whenever the need arises."

Dharmabuddhi agreed. Both went to their homes after burying a major portion of their wealth.

That night, Paapbuddhi went to the hiding place and dug out all the wealth. The next morning, he told Dharmabuddhi: "Friend! We have a large family to support. So we must bring our wealth."

Both went to the hiding place. When Dharmabuddhi found the wealth missing, he began wailing in grief. He was sure this was due to the craftiness of Paapbuddhi. He told Paapbuddhi: "Return my wealth, otherwise I will lodge a complaint with the king against you."

But Paapbuddhi falsely refuted the charge. Both began making charges and counter-charges. Ultimately, they went to the royal court to seek justice.

The presiding judge of the royal court asked them to take the oath. Paapbuddhi did not want to take the oath. He complained to the judge that this was not the appropriate way of dispensing justice and told him: "The norm is to examine the documentary proof first of all. In its absence, the judge should try to find out if there is any witness to that crime. Taking the oath is the last resort."

Continuing, Paapbuddhi said: "Vandevta (the forest deity) is our witness. Only he knows about the real culprit."

The courtiers were satisfied by his logic. All of them decided to make a request to the forest deity the next morning. Paapbuddhi then requested his father to go and conceal himself in the hollow of a shami (silk cotton) tree in the forest and advised him: "When they ask you about the culprit, mention the name of Dharmabuddhi."

The next morning, accompanied by all the courtiers and the judge, Paapbuddhi went to the forest. Standing before the shami tree, Paapbuddhi announced: "O deity of the forest, you know who the real culprit is. Tell us his name."

Sitting in the hollow of the shami tree, Paapbuddhi's father replied loudly: "Dharmabuddhi is the culprit. He has stolen all the wealth."

Everybody was amazed at this revelation. Dharmabuddhi was dumbstruck. He realised that Paapbuddhi might have hatched some conspiracy and decided to unearth it. Dharmabuddhi collected dry grass and twigs and piling them around the hollow in the tree, he made a big fire. After some time, the half-burnt father of Paapbuddhi emerged from the hollow. When he saw everybody looking at him in astonishment, he narrated the entire conspiracy. After revealing everything, he collapsed and died.

Insight: Foolish people often think they are very smart and don't hesitate to land their kith and kin in trouble with misplaced cunning. It is important to assess oneself and others accurately to perform effectively in life. Cheating by itself is bad enough and is made more despicable when one victimises a friend; this could end in tragedy, especially when the friend happens to be more intelligent. The excessively greedy and unscrupulous usually have to face the consequences — besides losing financially. Paapbuddhi was the cause of his father's painful death. The story warns us about insincere friendships and of the need to beware of unscrupulous cheats, lest we become unwitting accomplices by blindly trusting them and finally paying for their crimes.

Praising Dharmabuddhi, the judge decided to give him all the wealth and said: "*It is the duty of an intelligent man to consider both the negative and positive aspects of the means he applies;* otherwise he is certain to meet the same fate that befell the foolish heron."

Dharmabuddhi curiously asked: "What happened to the heron?"

The judge narrated the following story:

The Heron and the Snake

In a forest, there was a big banyan tree inhabited by numerous herons. A black cobra also lived in the hollow of the banyan tree, which would devour the eggs and chicks of the herons.

One day, a heron that had lost its chick to the cobra was wailing at the shore of a lake. A crab named Kulirak heard its wail. He asked: "O good heron! What happened? Why are you crying?"

The heron narrated all his woes and requested the crab to help him find a way to destroy the cobra.

Kulirak, the crab, had always regarded the heron as his enemy and was happy that the enemy was in trouble. He thought it would be better if the entire species of herons were destroyed. Thinking of a plan, he said: "Lay out all the bones of the fish you have eaten, from the burrow of the mongoose to the hollow in which the cobra lives.

The mongoose will reach that hollow following those bones and kill the cobra."

The heron liked this plan. He did as instructed by the crab, but the end result was no less catastrophic for him. Not only did the mongoose kill the cobra, he also devoured all the chicks as well as the eggs of the herons.

Insight: A man should thoroughly contemplate the negative consequences of his acts, before putting them into action. Compulsive behaviour when one thinks of only the motive and not the consequences can be catastrophic.

After completing his story, Karkat told Damanak: "You do not understand the repercussions your act of creating differences between Pingalak and Sanjeevak would have on you. *By causing injury to the master, you have shown your callousness. If you can do this to your master, you won't spare me either.* You are not trustworthy. Get lost! Go away from my sight! If it is possible for a rat to eat a thousand iron pieces, there would not be any doubt in a falcon's ability to lift a small child."

Observation: A person who is untrustworthy in one case could easily repeat his behaviour with other friends also; trusting such a person is a big risk, whether he is a colleague, your senior or junior.

Damanak curiously asked: "How and when did this happen?"

Karkat then narrated the following tale:

The Tale of an Iron Balance

A grocer's son named Jeernadhan lived in a city. Incidentally, he became very poor after incurring heavy losses in trade. Deciding to try his luck migrating to some other city, he thought: "The people of this city who have seen my prosperity will not hesitate to condemn me when they find me in such a bad condition."

Jeernadhan had an iron balance with him that weighed one thousand grams. Before migrating to another city, he decided to keep his iron balance as mortgage with a rich trader, on the promise that the trader would give it back to Jeernadhan on his return. The rich trader agreed to keep his iron balance.

After a long period, Jeernadhan returned and went to the rich trader to get back his iron balance. But the trader said: "I am sorry but your iron balance has been eaten by rats."

Jeernadhan realised that the trader was reluctant to return the balance and hence was playing a trick on him. He thought for a moment: "All right! What is the use of worrying about such a small matter? Can you allow your son to accompany me for a bath."

The rich trader agreed to send his son, Dhandena, with him. After a bath, Jeernadhan hid the trader's son inside a cave and closed its mouth with a large boulder. He then went to the trader's house. Seeing him alone, the trader asked: "Where is my son?"

Jeernadhan was waiting for this question and said: "I am sorry sir, while I was taking my bath, a large falcon picked up your son and flew away."

The rich trader blurted: "How can this happen? It is impossible!"

A quarrel erupted. Both went to the court to settle their dispute. The rich trader accused Jeernadhan of kidnapping his son. "Sir, this wretched Jeernadhan has abducted my son. He is not giving him back to me."

Jeernadhan replied: "Sir, if rats can eat an iron balance, can't a falcon fly away with a boy?"

Insight 1: Outrageous claims sometimes need to be handled with matching tactics especially when it comes to protecting yourself, your property and your rights. As a leader you may have to resort to such tactics to counter tall claims of those working under you.

The judge was amazed at this reply. He asked Jeernadhan to narrate the entire story clearly. Then, he ordered the rich trader to return the iron balance to Jeernadhan. The latter also handed over Dhandena back to the trader.

Completing his story, Karkat said: "Damanak! You are a jealous person. You were jealous of the favours Pingalak had been granting Sanjeevak. *It has rightly been said that a learned enemy is better than a foolish friend,* just like how a king was killed by his friend, a foolish monkey, and four Brahmins' lives were saved by a petty thief."

Damanak curiously asked about the story of the king and the monkey.

Karkat narrated the following tale:

The King and the Foolish Monkey

There was a king who had a pet monkey. The monkey did all kinds of work for the king. When the king slept, it would fan him. Once when the king was sleeping, the monkey saw a fly sitting on the king's chest. The monkey drove it away. But the fly returned and alighted on the king's nose. The monkey drove it away again. When this continued several times, the monkey was very irritated. He decided to kill the fly with a sword and get rid of this pest once for all.

The next time the monkey saw the fly sitting on the king's chest, he hit it with a powerful blow of the sword. The sword did not even graze the fly, which flew away, but the king was killed instantly.

appropriate for the threat. If a matchbox catches fire, we need not call the fire brigade! If such basic common sense is lacking, we risk endangering ourselves and those around us.

Having told Damanak this tale, Karkat then narrated the story of the Brahmins and a thief:

The Brahmins and a Thief

A learned Brahmin lived in a city, but because of bad deeds committed in his previous birth, he became a thief. One day, he saw four Brahmins who had come to trade goods. The thief decided to steal their belongings.

He went to them and impressed the four with his knowledge. The Brahmins were pleased with him and appointed him as their attendant.

Some time later, the Brahmins decided to return to their native place. They sold whatever they had and purchased jewels. The thief had not been successful so far in his attempts to rob them, so he grew anxious when he learnt about their plan to wind-up their business. He was not ready to let them go till his objective was fulfilled and requested: "O learned Brahmins! Living in your company, I have developed an attachment towards you all. I cannot bear a separation. I wish to go along with you all."

The Brahmins agreed to take him along. On their return journey, the Brahmins had concealed the jewels under their dhotis. While they were passing by a village named Pallipur, some crows saw them. These crows were in fact accomplices of Bhils who robbed passers-by. They began cawing: "O Bhils! Come soon! Come soon! There are four Brahmins carrying a lot of jewels with them. Snatch their wealth!"

The Bhils chased the Brahmins, beat them with sticks and disrobed them. When they did not find anything, they were puzzled. But they had full faith in the crows. So the Bhils warned the Brahmins to surrender all in their possession, otherwise they would be killed.

The thief got scared as he thought he would be killed after the Brahmins. He thought: 'If this happens, I will not get the wealth! Moreover, these poor Brahmins will be killed. Instead, if I save their lives by sacrificing my own, I will attain heaven.'

The thief told the Bhils: "If you do not believe the Brahmins' words, you can verify the truth by killing me first."

The Bhils killed the thief but did not find any wealth, so they spared the Brahmins' lives.

While Karkat was narrating this story to Damanak, Sanjeevak – who was seriously injured by the assault from Pingalak – fell flat on the ground. Suspecting him to be dead, Pingalak was dejected. He started cursing himself: "I have committed an unpardonable sin by killing Sanjeevak. I have committed treachery against him."

Damanak was very happy that Sanjeevak was dead and now the path was clear for him to become the minister. He consoled Pingalak: "Is justifiable for a king to mourn the death of a mean creature like a bird or an ox, who was harbouring malice and enmity towards him? It has been said in the Scriptures that one should not even hesitate to kill one's wife, son, father or friend, if there is a threat to his life from any of them."

Pingalak was satisfied with Damanak's explanation. He appointed him as his minister, a post that Damanak coveted.

Insight: Flattery and corruption are not new issues or peculiar to our times. Climbing the career ladder by stepping on others' toes and lives has been common practice for millennia. The story reminds us that however popular the practice, it cannot be condoned. The seriousness of moral degradation is not mitigated by the fact that many people have done the same thing before us.

The Second Tantra – Mitrasamprapti

There was a city named Mahilaropya in the southern part of India. Near the city there was a large banyan tree. Innumerable birds fed on its fruits. The hollow of its trunk was filled with worms and insects. Travellers passing by the tree would rest in its shade.

Laghupatnak – the Crow

A crow named Laghupatnak lived on the banyan tree. One day while flying towards the city, he saw a fowler heading towards the banyan tree. The fowler was carrying a net and his intentions obviously were not good.

The crow feared for the lives of the birds living on the banyan tree. Flying back to the banyan tree, he warned the birds about the fowler's arrival, saying: "The fowler will sprinkle rice grains all around the tree to trap you. Do not fall into his trap."

In the meantime, the fowler arrived. He sprinkled rice grains all around the banyan tree and hid behind a bush, waiting for the birds. But all the birds remained at their positions and evinced no interest in the grains.

Right then, the king of the pigeons, Chitragreeva, arrived accompanied by his flock. Laghupatnak warned him also but he did not pay heed to this. As a result, all the pigeons were trapped in the fowler's net.

When the fowler saw the pigeons trapped in his net, he ran towards it to catch the trapped birds. Chitragreeva advised the other pigeons to remain calm. Because *only a man of unwavering intelligence can come out of a calamity successfully.*

Chitragreeva advised all the pigeons to fly along with the net. "We will try to free ourselves from this net as soon as we are out of his sight," said Chitragreeva.

All the pigeons followed his instruction and flew away. The fowler followed them, thinking that very soon the pigeons would start quarrelling among themselves and fall down. But this did not happen and the fowler returned to his home with a sullen face. He had not only lost the birds, but also his net, which was his means of livelihood.

When Chitragreeva saw that the fowler was not following them, he advised all the pigeons to fly towards Mahilaropya where his friend Hiranyak the mouse lived, who would free them from the net by cutting it with his sharp teeth. Hiranyak the mouse lived safely in his burrow, which had a thousand openings and resembled a fort.

Reaching the burrow, Chitragreeva called out to Hiranyak. Hiranyak rushed out of his burrow when he heard Chitragreeva's voice. He wanted to free Chitragreeva first, but Chitragreeva forbade him from doing so, because *he wanted the other pigeons to be freed before himself. He said: "Hiranyak! As the king, I have a responsibility towards my subjects.* Suppose, while freeing me, your teeth are broken, my subjects would remain trapped in the net. If this happens, I would certainly go to hell."

Hiranyak was very pleased with his friend's sense of duty and responsibility. He freed all the pigeons first and then Chitragreeva at the end.

Laghupatnak the crow was flying behind the pigeons trapped in the net, curious to know the final outcome. He was amazed to see all the pigeons being freed from the net. He was very impressed with Hiranyak and wanted to make friends with him.

Insight: Group action is more powerful than individual action. If you want to succeed, join like-minded associations whose members are professionally or goal linked.

Laghupatnak called out to Hiranyak imitating the voice of Chitragreeva. Hiranyak thought that perhaps Chitragreeva was calling him again. He peeped from his burrow but when he saw somebody else, he asked: "Who are you?"

Laghupatnak introduced himself and expressed his desire for friendship with him. But Hiranyak refused to be friends with him because crows and mice are natural enemies.

Laghupatnak then told Hiranyak: *"Learned men become friends if they pronounce just seven verses together or if they walk seven steps together. I have come to your place to be your friend. If you do not want to come before me, just assure me that you will talk to me, whenever I come here. I will be satisfied even with this."*

Considering Laghupatnak to be a truthful scholar, Hiranyak at last agreed to be his friend but warned him against entering his burrow. The crow agreed.

In due course, both became very good friends. They used to converse, exchange their food, etc. Yet, their friendship was superficial. After some days the mouse had developed such faith in the crow that he would talk to him sitting in the shade of his outstretched wings.

One day, tears in his eyes, Laghupatnak told Hiranyak: "Friend! I will no longer stay at this place because I have become disenchanted with it."

Hiranyak asked the reason for his disenchantment. Laghupatnak replied that the place was severely affected by famine and it had become difficult for him to survive. Hiranyak asked him where he intended to go.

Laghupatnak replied: "My best friend Mantharak, a tortoise, lives in a deep lake situated in a dense forest. Mantharak will provide me with fish every day and this way I could pass my time happily."

Hiranyak expressed his desire to go along with him, claiming that he too was facing severe hardships here. Laghupatnak wondered how he could take Hiranyak along with him: "How can you come along with me? You do not know how to fly."

Hiranyak asked Laghupatnak to carry him on his back. Laghupatnak was very proud of his flying skills and agreed to carry Hiranyak on his back. Hiranyak swiftly climbed onto his back.

Laghupatnak flew towards the lake, where Mantharak lived.

When Mantharak saw this extraordinary crow carrying a mouse on his back, he was frightened and entered the water. Laghupatnak hid the mouse in the hollow of a tree and went to meet Mantharak, calling out to him.

Recognising the voice of his friend, Mantharak emerged. Both were very pleased to see each other. Mantharak then asked him about Hiranyak: "Who was that mouse sitting on your back? A mouse being the natural enemy of a crow, how was it possible for you to befriend him?"

Laghupatnak told him the mouse was his friend Hiranyak. In the meantime, Hiranyak arrived and after greeting Mantharak sat quietly. Introducing Hiranyak to Mantharak, Laghupatnak said: "The seemingly small Hiranyak has many great qualities. He too is disenchanted like me."

Insight: If two or more persons are like-minded and share common interests, the two attributes can become strong business bonds. If you admire someone greatly for his qualities, you will not bother about his caste, creed or race but try to draw him into your circle and if the attraction and admiration is mutual, it will be a great match and most likely achieve a lot that is worthwhile, together. By being aware of this fact, we can use it as a guideline to build our circle of friends and acquaintances and choose the people who work under us.

Observation: The greatness of a leader lies in his inherent character traits and cultivated abilities, not in his physical personality.

Mantharak asked why Hiranyak was disenchanted. Hiranyak narrated the following story:

The Hermit and the Mouse

In a big city in south India, there was a temple of Lord Mahadeva where a hermit named Tamrachurna lived.

Everyday he went around the city streets begging for alms and collected a sufficient amount to satisfy his hunger. Daily, after eating his fill, he kept the leftovers at a height, out of reach of dogs and cats. In the morning, he would give this food to his attendants and followers.

At this time, I too was living in the temple. One day, my friends informed me about the foodstuff, which the hermit kept at a height for safety. They sought my help in getting the foodstuff.

I went along with my friends to this place and in a single leap I scaled the height where the foodstuff was kept. I first allowed my friends to satisfy their hunger and I ate in the end. Since then, this became our daily routine.

When the hermit discovered this, he procured a bamboo stick to hit the bowl in which the foodstuff was kept, even while sleeping. This scared us and we were no longer able to relish the leftovers.

One day a friend of Tamrachurna arrived, whose name was Vrihatspik. He was on a pilgrimage. Tamrachurna treated his friend very well. In the night, his friend began preaching to Tamrachurna on various religious matters. But Tamrachurna's entire attention was focussed on protecting the foodstuff.

When his friend realised Tamrachurna was not attentive, he angrily said: "O Tamrachurna! I have realised that you are not worthy of being called a friend, you are arrogant."

Tamrachurna was afraid that his friend had misunderstood him and revealed the real reason behind his inattentiveness: "Friend! These mice are giving me lot of trouble. They eat the foodstuff, no matter how high I keep the bowl. So I was just trying to drive them away by making noise with this bamboo stick."

Insight 1: Stress and tension don't allow you to concentrate on a task or on what somebody is saying; such inattentiveness may be misread as arrogance or lack of commitment. So first work on getting rid of or controlling stress-causing problems; only then can you expect to perform well in your undertakings. A relaxed and stress-free lifestyle (which some well-to-do and

well-organised people achieve) can improve your appearance;
hence the ancient belief that the 'heat' emanating from jewels
can increase the glow and radiance of a person.

Insight 2: When saturated with worldly pursuits it is not possible
to attain any spiritual advancement. However, for a well-
rounded personality, we need to take an interest in both the
material and spiritual planes, without allowing worldly affairs
to monopolise our mind and time. A well-rounded person would
naturally be a better leader.

Vrihatspik asked him whether he knew where the hole of the mouse was. When Tamrachurna replied in the negative, his friend said the mice must have been living somewhere in the vicinity of a storehouse in which jewels and ornaments were stored. "This is the reason why the mice could jump and reach that height, because the 'heat' emanating from the wealth increases the glow and radiance of a living being."

Then Vrihatspik mentioned the story of a woman named Shandili who wanted to exchange winnowed sesame seeds for unwinnowed ones. Tamrachurna was amazed that one could be so foolish as to exchange unwinnowed sesame seeds for winnowed ones. He was eager to hear the story...

The Greedy Jackal

A Bhil lived in a forest region. One day when he went to hunt, he saw a huge boar and shot it with his bow. The injured boar attacked him and tore his abdomen apart. Later, the Bhil and the boar succumbed to their injuries.

Right then, a jackal arrived, wandering in search of food. He was happy to see the dead bodies of the Bhil and the boar and felt that God had been very kind to him.

But there was one problem. The Bhil's bow was also lying there and the jackal wished to relish all that he found. Even the leather string of the bow seemed like a good appetiser, so the greedy jackal thought of eating the string of the bow first. An arrow was still stuck on the string of the fully charged bow, in a 'ready-to-shoot' position.

As soon as the jackal nibbled the string, it snapped and the arrow pierced his head. The greedy jackal died instantly.

Insight: Greed clouds judgement and is dangerous for your well-being. Sadly, such mental aberrations very often negate what gracious fate offers by blinding us to its bounty. As a leader, you are more exposed to such temptations; to steer clear of it all you should never let your guard down.

Hiranyak then narrated another tale...

Praptvyamarth
– the Grocer's Son

Once, I had gone to perform some religious rites. It was the rainy season. I requested a Brahmin to allow me to stay in his house for some days, to which he agreed.

I stayed at his home, keeping myself busy in the worship of deities. One morning, I heard the Brahmin telling his wife: "Tomorrow being Dakshinayan Sankranti, it is considered the most auspicious day for donations. I have decided to go to a nearby village to seek alms. You too must feed a Brahmin."

The Brahmin's wife was very angry, since there was nothing in their home. She said: "It was my misfortune that I married you. Since then, I have never had joy and happiness in my life."

But the Brahmin convinced his wife, explaining the importance of donations made on Dakshinayan Sankranti. He also advised her on the negative aspects of excessive desire and narrated the following story:

A grocer named Sagardutt lived in a city. One day, his son purchased a book for a hundred rupees in which it was written: "A man gets whatever is written in his destiny."

Sagardutt was very angry that his son had purchased a book for hundred rupees in which only one sentence was written. Admonishing his son that he could never earn money in his life, the grocer drove him out of the house.

His son migrated to another city and began living there. When people asked him who he was, he replied that he was "PRAPTVYAMARTHAM LABHATE MANUSHYAM".

So people called him Praptvyamarth.

One day, a princess who had come to attend a festival saw him and was infatuated by his handsome appearance. She intimated a friend about her feelings. Her friend went to Praptvyamarth and told him about the feelings of the princess towards him. She also said that the princess would die if he did not meet her. Praptvyamarth asked how he could meet the princess.

She replied: "Come to the palace at night. You will find a rope hanging down the palace wall. You can climb up holding the rope and enter the palace."

Praptvyamarth said: "All right."

When she went back, Praptvyamarth thought it would not be proper to go because – 'One who makes love to the wife of his teacher, wife of his friend, wife of his master and wife of his servant, goes to hell'.

But it was in his destiny to meet the princess. As he was loitering around, he accidentally passed by the palace and saw a rope hanging down. He climbed up with the rope. When the princess saw him, she felt very happy. She treated him with all respect and seated him on

her bed, saying: "Since the day I saw you, I have chosen you as my husband. Now I cannot even think of marrying anybody else."

But Praptvyamarth did not reply. The princess forced him to say something. He simply said: "A man gets whatever is written in his destiny."

The princess thought that perhaps this man was somebody else and sent him back.

On the way, Praptvyamarth saw an old temple and, feeling tired, he slept there. By chance, the police officer of that city arrived there to meet his beloved. When he saw Praptvyamarth sleeping there, he asked him to sleep on his bed, fearing that his secret love affairs would be disclosed. Praptvyamarth went away but by mistake he slept on another bed.

The police officer's daughter, Satyavati, was also sleeping on the same bed waiting for her lover. She thought that her lover had arrived and was very happy. But Praptvyamarth kept quiet. When she coaxed him to say something, he said: "A man gets whatever is written in his destiny."

She became angry and drove him out. While Praptvyamarth was going out, he saw a marriage procession. He mingled with the group. Hardly had the marriage procession reached the bride's house, when an elephant in rut arrived there. Everybody ran helter-skelter. Thinking that the bride might be alone, Praptvyamarth rushed to protect her. He told her not to be afraid and held her right hand. Suddenly, the elephant approached. Praptvyamarth shouted loudly at the elephant. Luckily, it went away.

After the elephant had gone, the bridegroom returned along with the marriage party. When the bridegroom saw Praptvyamarth holding the hand of the bride, he asked the bride's father: "You had promised to marry your daughter to me. So who is this fellow holding her hand?"

The bride's father asked his daughter. She replied that he was her saviour and she was going to marry him: "I can never marry the man who ran away, leaving me to die."

A commotion erupted amongst them. The king was passing through that place accompanied by the princess. The king asked Praptvyamarth to narrate the entire story. He said: "A man gets whatever is written in his destiny."

After thinking for a while, the princess said: "Even God is incapable of changing that."

Then the police officer's daughter said: "For this reason nothing makes me sorrowful and I am not amazed by anything."

At last the bride said: "Whatever is mine others cannot claim."

The king then asked all the assembled people to narrate their stories separately. When he heard the facts, he was very pleased with Praptvyamarth and at once married the princess to him. Praptvyamarth also invited his parents over and lived happily thereafter.

Having narrated the story, Hiranyak said: "A man gets whatever is written in his destiny. Perhaps being disenchanted with this world was in my destiny and this friend has brought me to you."

Observation: Is destiny preordained or does one mould it through talent, hard work and opportunities? If any of these factors were different wouldn't one's destiny also differ? For example, if the groom had tried to protect the bride from the elephant, wouldn't she have married him rather than a stranger?

Mantharak said: "Indeed, Laghupatnak is your friend. Despite being hungry he did not eat you."

Mantharak then told Hiranyak to live near the lake, leaving behind all his worries and woes. He said: *"Wealth, youth, wife and ripe cereals do not remain with you forever."*

This story helped the Brahmin's wife understand the point. She agreed to make a donation the next day and decided to donate laddus. Satisfied with her resolution, the Brahmin went away.

The Brahmin's wife soaked winnowed sesame seeds in water and kept this under the sun to dry. Suddenly, a dog appeared and urinated on the sesame seeds. The Brahmin's wife was upset. She decided to exchange these seeds with somebody. She felt anybody would like to exchange her winnowed sesame seeds with unwinnowed ones.

She went to the same houses where I had gone to beg for alms, saying: "Exchange your unwinnowed sesame seeds with my winnowed ones."

The housewife residing in one house was happy she was receiving winnowed sesame seeds and would be relieved from the task of winnowing her sesame seeds. She went inside to fetch her unwinnowed sesame seeds.

The housewife's son stopped her: "Mother! According to the policies stated by Kamand, unwinnowed sesame seeds must not be exchanged with winnowed ones. There must be a reason behind her decision to exchange winnowed sesame seeds with unwinnowed ones."

Insight: A show of undue generosity should arouse suspicion. If you ignore it, you could be cheated just like the housewife would have been cheated by Shandili had her son not intervened. The housewife got the point and refused to exchange her unwinnowed sesame seeds with the winnowed ones.

After completing his story, Vrihatspik asked Tamrachurna if he was aware of the route the mouse had taken. Tamrachurna replied that the mouse was never alone but accompanied by other mice. Vrihatspik then asked for a spade and said: "Early morning tomorrow before people awake, we will follow in the footsteps of the mice and reach the place where they live."

Hiranyak continued narrating his story...

I was amazed by his intelligence. I was also worried about the safety of our burrow. I decided to abandon my hole along with my companions and we left the place.

While we were coming out of our burrow, a cat jumped on us and killed many. Some of my companions returned to the same hole, cursing me. Others were badly injured. I also returned to our burrow.

Vrihatspik followed the stains of blood and reached our burrow. He took the jewels from there, sitting upon which I used to enjoy myself and that had enabled me to make those tremendous leaps.

When Vrihatspik left after ransacking our burrow, some of my companions occupied it again. In the night, as usual they began trying to jump up to the bowl. Being aware of our presence, Tamrachurna began hitting the bowl with his bamboo stick, but Vrihatspik asked him not to worry as the reason behind the ability of the mouse to jump so high had been removed.

Which was true. Despite trying hard, I remained unsuccessful in my attempts to reach the bowl. Consequently, my companions stopped respecting me and abandoned me since I had become poor and powerless. So I decided to retrieve the jewels from Tamrachurna's possession.

Tamrachurna kept the jewels in a box, which he used as a pillow while sleeping. I went to the place where Tamrachurna was sleeping and began to cut the box with my sharp teeth. The sound awoke him. He hit me with the bamboo stick, but luckily I escaped unhurt.

After narrating the story, Hiranyak said: "A man is certain to get whatever is in his destiny. Even the deities are incapable of changing that. Therefore, nothing makes me feel sorry or wonder because I will acquire whatever is mine according to my destiny and nobody can change that."

Then Mantharak mentioned the tale of Somilak, a foolish man who could not enjoy his wealth because it was not in his destiny.

Hiranyak was curious to know about this story. Mantharak narrated the following story:

Somilak – the Weaver

There once lived a weaver named Somilak. Despite being an expert weaver he did not receive proper remuneration or rewards. One day Somilak told his wife he would go to some other place to try his luck as he was not being properly rewarded for his work here. He reasoned: "Weavers who are less efficient have become richer, whereas even after being so proficient in my work I remain poor."

His wife did not agree with him and said that perhaps it was in their destiny to remain poor: "We are just reaping the fruits of our past lives. Your decision of going to an alien place is not proper."

But the weaver had made up his mind. So, one day, he left for another city named Vardhamanpur. He stayed there for three years and earned three hundred gold coins. He then decided to return to his native place. While he was passing through a forest, darkness fell. He climbed up a banyan tree for safety and fell asleep. In his sleep, he dreamt about two men who were talking to each other.

One man said: "O Kartah! You know this Somilak has only so much wealth in his destiny that is required for survival. Then why did you give him three hundred gold coins?"

The second man replied: "O Karman! It is my duty to give wealth to a hardworking person. It depends only upon you, whether you allow it to remain in his possession or not."

Somilak then woke up from his sleep. He found that the gold coins had vanished. He became very sad. Instead of returning to his native place, he decided to go back to the same city. Within a year, he had earned five hundred gold coins. So he proceeded towards his native place. Fearful of losing his gold coins, he kept walking and did not take rest. While he was passing through the same forest, he met two persons who resembled the duo he had seen in the dream.

One of them was saying: "O Kartah! Why did you give him five hundred gold coins? Don't you know he has only such amount of wealth in his destiny as is required for survival."

The other replied: "O Karman! It is my duty to give wealth to a hardworking man. Now it is up to you whether you allow it to remain in his possession or not."

When Somilak heard their conversation, he was afraid and opened his bundle to check whether the gold coins were safe or not. All the coins had vanished!

Disheartened, Somilak decided to end his life. He went near a tree and as he was about to put a noose around his neck, he heard a voice: "Somilak! Do not take your life. I am the one who has stolen your wealth. I will not allow more wealth than what you need for your survival. You better go back home. But since you are fortunate enough to have had a visitation from me, you can ask for any boon."

Somilak wanted his gold coins returned, but the unseen voice refused outright, saying: "You are not destined to enjoy the pleasure of wealth. What is the use of giving it to you?"

Yet Somilak insisted: "Even if a man is born in a low caste or is abandoned by his people, if he has wealth people respect him. It does not make any difference to them even if he is a miser."

The unseen voice then instructed Somilak to return to Vardhamanpur, where he would meet two sons of a grocer. Their names were Guptadhan and Upabhuktadhan. *Try to understand their real nature and you will certainly receive whatever you demand,* the voice said.

Observation: Somilak is instructed to understand the nature of these two brothers, which are contrasting. We may consider these voices as his intuition or divine guidance and at the end of the story we realise why it was necessary for Somilak to understand these two people.

Somilak returned to Vardhamanpur. First, he went to Guptadhan's house. Guptadhan misbehaved and drove him out of his house. Yet Somilak forcibly entered his house. At night, when Guptadhan was having dinner with his family, he rudely gave some food to Somilak. Somilak meekly ate whatever was given and went to sleep.

At midnight, Somilak heard a voice. He tried to overhear what was being said: "O Kartah! You have caused excessive expenditure to Guptadhan. He had to feed Somilak. How will he recover his losses?"

The other voice replied: "O Karman! It is my duty to benefit people. The end result lies in your hand."

When Guptadhan woke up the next morning, he had to fast for the entire day as he was suffering from indigestion. This way he recovered his losses. Somilak then went to Upabhuktadhan's house, where he was treated very well. A lot of money was spent on treating him.

At midnight, Somilak heard the same conversation: "Kartah! How will Upabhuktadhan recover his losses incurred by spending lavishly on his guest."

The other voice replied: "Karman! This was my duty. The final result lies in your hand."

In the morning, the king's envoy arrived with many presents and prizes sent by the king. Somilak understood that charitable Upabhuktadhan was far better than Guptadhan the miser. He wished he could become just like Upabhuktadhan.

Observation: Somilak was forced to think about the contrasting behaviour of the two brothers and on exercising his judgement realised that it is far better to be charitable than to be a miser. This was probably the maturity he needed to unlock his good fortune.

After completing his story Mantharak said: "Hiranyak! *You too should not worry about wealth. Wealth that cannot be used is good for nothing.*"

Insight 1: The voices Somilak heard and his dreams could be compared to his conscience, which told him that the pursuit of wealth alone was no good. The voices finally imparted a lesson by directing him to meet two brothers who had contrasting natures and from whose behaviour he learnt a valuable lesson

in life: It is far better to be charitable than to be a miser and
think all the time about how to recover your losses. By being
charitable and helping those in need, goodwill is created, and
good relationships have their own rewards.

Insight 2: *Perform your task well and don't worry about the*
results. Destiny will provide whatever is due to you. Worry is
useless and counterproductive. Excessive worry about destiny
may not allow you to enjoy even what destiny has given you!

Insight 3: *Succumbing to negative thoughts and expressing*
them not only negatively affects our outlook in life, but it also
affects the people we deal with. The weaver's wife doubted
whether they were destined to enjoy wealth. This belief haunted
the husband even after he migrated and he was robbed of his
wealth time and again. As a leader you have to be even more
alert to remain positive because others look up to you and you
unconsciously influence them.

While Mantharak was extolling the virtues of charity, contentment
and the like to Hiranyak, a deer suddenly came rushing and entered
the lake. His sudden arrival had scared Laghupatnak. He flew away
and perched high on a tree. Hiranyak too hid behind a bush. And
Mantharak dived into the lake. Then Laghupatnak felt it was only a
thirsty deer come to quench his thirst and called out to Mantharak
and Hiranyak to come out from hiding.

But when Mantharak saw the terrified deer, he realised that it was
under some kind of threat and said so to Laghupatnak. The deer said
that he was indeed running away from hunters who had killed many
of his friends. He requested them to shelter him, which they did.
Chitrang, the deer, thereafter began living with them.

One day, Chitrang wasn't around. So Laghupatnak flew in search of
him. He saw Chitrang trapped in a net. After consoling him, he took
Hiranyak to that place. Mantharak too followed them. Hiranyak cut
the net with his sharp teeth and Chitrang escaped. Laghupatnak also
flew away, but poor Mantharak was not that lucky. The hunter had
arrived by then. When he saw that Chitrang had escaped, he was
furious. Suddenly, he spied Mantharak, the tortoise, trying to escape.
The hunter caught him and proceeded towards his home, having
fastened Mantharak inside the net.

When Laghupatnak, Hiranyak and Chitrang saw that Mantharak had been caught by the hunter, they planned to rescue him. According to the plan, Chitrang feigned death by the side of a lake. Laghupatnak, the crow, began pecking Chitrang's head. When the hunter saw this, mistaking Chitrang to be dead, he put Mantharak down on the ground, thinking that as he was fastened he could not run away and proceeded to procure the deer.

Meanwhile, Hiranyak swiftly cut the net and released Mantharak, who quickly entered the lake. As the hunter approached Chitrang, he got up and fled. All of them then ran away. Dejected, the hunter cursed his fate and returned home after having lost everything.

Insight: Befriend a network of people with diverse talents and abilities. This will be a great support for each one in diverse situations. Just as you receive support from others, you too will have the pleasure of helping others in your circle. If you generously allow new people to join your circle, your power will increase, as they too will contribute their mite for the group's welfare.

The Third Tantra — Kakolukiyam

There was a very big banyan tree near the city named Mahilaropya in southern India. On that tree lived Meghavarna — the king of the crows — and other crows. Nearby there was a mountain with a cave in which lived Arimardan — the king of the owls – and his family members.

Both the kings had great hostility towards each other. Arimardan would wander around the banyan tree at night and kill whatever crows he found. In this way, he had killed many crows.

One day Meghavarna called a meeting in which all his ministers were present. He said: "Our enemy is powerful and cruel. He also recognises the value of time. He always attacks us during the night, because he knows we cannot see then. We also don't know the owls' residence, otherwise we would have attacked them during the daytime. So what should we do now?"

The ministers advised him to arrange a private meeting with the king owl, so that the reason for the enmity could be known. Meghavarna then consulted his five chief ministers separately on what should be done. A minister named Ujjivi said it was not appropriate to fight with a powerful enemy. "So we must have a reconciliation with him," said Ujjivi.

Meghavarna then consulted his second minister, Sanjivi, about his opinion. Sanjivi was against any kind of reconciliation with the enemy as it was against morality. "We must fight such an enemy," said Sanjivi.

On being asked for his opinion, the third minister, Anujivi said: "We should neither fight with the enemy nor have a reconciliation. We should attack the enemy only when he is docile. This policy is known as 'Yan'."

Then Meghavarna asked Prajivi for his opinion. Prajivi said: "Neither should we fight nor should we reconcile. Attacking the enemy when he is in distress does not seem logical to me. I think 'Asan' will be the right policy for us. As soon as the enemy attacks, we must remain inside our fort and try to organise ourselves."

When Meghavarna asked his fifth minister, Chiranjivi, for his opinion, he replied: "We must seek help from others."

At last, Meghavarna asked his most senior minister, Sthirjivi, who was a minister during his father's reign too, about his opinion. Sthirjivi said: "Though whatever has been said by all the ministers is correct in special circumstances, yet I feel that, at the moment, the policy of 'Dvaidhibhav' would be most appropriate. According to this policy, we must maintain false friendship and enmity alternately with the enemy so that he gets confused."

Sthirjivi then instructed Meghavarna to find out any weakness of his enemy. Meghavarna replied that he was unaware of any such weakness.

Sthirjivi told him not to worry, as his detectives would find out the weak points of the enemy.

Meghavarna then asked him when the enmity between crows and owls began. Sthirjivi narrated the following tale:

Once upon a time, all the birds like the swan, parrot, heron, cuckoo, owl, peacock, pigeon, cock et al. had decided to choose another king, as their king Garuda was always busy attending to Lord Vishnu.

They selected the owl as their king and began making arrangements for his coronation. Just as the owl was about to occupy the throne, a crow arrived unannounced. All the birds thought that the crow, being shrewd, would make a better choice.

The crow was surprised to see the gathering of birds and inquired about the reason. When he heard that they had elected the owl as their king, he told them: "It is a pity that you have elected this ugly creature to rule you as your king, despite the presence of beautiful birds like the peacock, the swan et al. who are more capable. Earlier, Garuda was our king and his name was enough to terrify enemies. The name of his successor should also be capable of arousing terror in the hearts of enemies."

Insight: Creating obstacles to thwart the prospects of others out of jealousy or self-interest can cause deep hatred and enmity for life or even generations. It is wiser to work for your own success without putting others down. In this way, whenever you achieve success, the satisfaction is greater because you worked for it and the fruits of your labour may come much faster because you did not waste energy to plot or fight a rival. If you develop a helpful disposition and prove yourself through selfless service, you will be a natural leader of the pack and most likely be elected to the top post.

Pausing, the crow then continued: "Electing the owl as our king will not serve any purpose, just as even the rabbit gets excited simply hearing the name of the Moon and hops about happily."

All the birds asked: "How come?"

The crow narrated the following story:

Chaturdant, the Elephant and Lambakarn, the Rabbit

A huge elephant named Chaturdant once lived in a forest. He was the king of all the elephants. Once due to prolonged drought, all the lakes in the forest dried up. So all the elephants requested Chaturdant to find a way out.

Chaturdant led all the elephants to a lake, which had water throughout the year. After travelling for five days, the herd reached the lake, exhausted and thirsty. So they first quenched their thirst. This done, they began to play in the water.

On the shore of the lake lived many rabbits who had dug their burrows in the soft soil. During their play, the elephants trampled many rabbits and destroyed their burrows. Many rabbits also lost their limbs.

When the elephants went away, the rabbits assembled and considered the fact that since there was no water in other lakes, the elephants were sure to return here and kill many more rabbits by trampling them. The more they considered it, the graver the problem appeared.

77

At last, they devised a plan, according to which the most intelligent among them, Lambakarn, was to be sent as an emissary to the king of the elephants.

Lambakarn proceeded via the same path through which the elephants were expected to arrive. He climbed up a big tree and waited. After some time, he saw the king of the elephants coming. He said: "O wicked elephant! How dare you trample the loved ones of the Moon deity! Since you have killed many rabbits, the Moon deity is very angry with you."

The elephant was astonished and asked who he was. The rabbit replied: "My name is Lambakarn. I am the envoy of the Moon deity. I live in Chandraloka. The Moon has sent me to warn you."

The elephant curiously asked about the whereabouts of the Moon deity. The rabbit replied that the Moon was in the lake, where it had come to enquire about the well-being of the rabbits.

The elephant expressed a desire to meet the Moon. The rabbit took him to the lake. In the water of the lake the elephant saw a reflection of the Moon. He was convinced about the authenticity of the rabbit's tale. The elephant then went back and never returned.

Completing his story, the crow said: "This is the reason why I say that just the name of a great person is enough to ensure a problem-free life."

Insight: Name-dropping can come in handy when faced with an insurmountable problem. Or, without dropping any names, even if you behave as though you have great contacts, you may achieve some results in real life too and rid yourself of tormentors.

"*A person who wants to live happily must never choose a master who is mean, lazy and an addict,* otherwise he will meet the same fate as a rabbit and a bird met when they were destroyed by a mean counsellor," said the crow.

All the birds wanted to hear this story, so the crow narrated the following tale...

The Rabbit and the Bird

Earlier, I used to live on a tree. In the hollow of the same tree there also lived a bird named Kapinjal. Both of us were great friends. We would have discussions on various topics such as spiritual and religious matters. One evening, Kapinjal did not return home and I was very anxious about his safety. When he did not return even after many days, I was sure he was no more.

Finding the hollow empty, one day a rabbit began living there. I did not object, being happy that I would get a chance to make friends with him. I was very surprised to see Kapinjal return one day. He seemed very healthy and was looking very good. He was very sad to see the rabbit occupying his home. He requested the rabbit to vacate his home, but the rabbit refused.

When they realised it was beyond them to resolve their dispute, they decided to seek the advice of a religious person. A cat was listening to them. He swiftly picked some Kush grass and arrived at the shore of a lake. He raised his forearms and looking at the Sun began mouthing these words: "This world is meaningless. Relatives are companions for a temporary period. Life itself is impermanent, therefore one must try to follow the path of virtuosity."

When both of them heard the cat chanting such sacred words, they thought he would be the best judge to settle their dispute.

Kapinjal requested the rabbit to seek the cat's advice. The rabbit narrated the tale of their dispute. The cat said that as he was old, he could not hear properly. He requested them to repeat everything in his ears loudly. Both the bird and the rabbit fell into the cat's trap. As soon as they approached the cat, it killed and devoured them at once.

Insight: Wouldn't it have been wiser for the rabbit and the bird to settle their dispute amicably? Seeking justice from the courts for non-essential issues can very often ruin us physically, mentally and financially, much like the cat devoured the two quarrelling parties.

After completing his story, the crow again warned the birds against electing the owl as their king. All the birds were convinced that the owl was not fit to be their king.

The owl, who had already occupied the throne, was waiting for the moment when the birds would crown him king. One of his informants told him about the hurdles put up by the crow. The owl angrily went towards the crow and asked why he had stymied his coronation.

The crow too regretted he had developed unwanted enmity with the owl. Since that day, the owl has been a sworn enemy of crows.

Insight: Think before you act. Once you acquire an enemy by thoughtless speech, it may not be easy to patch up. Careful thought rather than impulsive action is worth the pain. The lesson we learn is useful for all and even more so for leaders, because you cannot be a leader if you have only enemies and no followers!

After hearing this story, Meghavarna asked: "What should we do now?"

The old minister replied that he himself would go to the enemy's place and kill him by deception. He said: "*Even the most intelligent and powerful man can be defeated with the help of deceptive tactics,* just like in the case of the Brahmin whose goat was deceitfully taken by cheats."

Meghavarna wanted to know how tricksters had cheated the Brahmin. The old minister narrated the following story:

The Brahmin and the Cheats

A Brahmin named Mitra Sharma lived in a village. One day he went to his host's house to perform oblation. His host gave him a very healthy goat as dakshina after the oblation. The Brahmin carried the goat on his shoulders and proceeded homeward. Three cheats saw the Brahmin coming and decided to steal his goat.

One of them approached Mitra Sharma and said: "O Brahmin! Being a Brahmin, it is not proper for you to carry a dog like this. You will become impure from the dog's touch."

Mitra Sharma became angry: "You fool! Don't you see I am carrying a goat and not a dog!"

The first cheat replied: "Don't be angry. I have only spoken the truth."

Mitra Sharma resumed his journey. He then met the second cheat who was waiting for him. The second cheat said: "O Brahmin! Why are you carrying a dead calf on your shoulder?"

Mitra Sharma replied that it was a goat and not a dead calf. Walking ahead, Mitra Sharma met the third cheat, who said: "Why are you carrying a donkey on your shoulder?"

Now, Mitra Sharma was confused. Throwing the goat down, he walked away. The three cheats had a grand feast that day.

Insight: It was impulsive action that deprived the Brahmin of his goat. The deceptive tactics of the cheats worked due to proper planning and also because the Brahmin acted without thinking.

Completing the story, the old minister said: "*One should not have enmity even with small creatures who are united,* otherwise he would meet the same fate of the snake who was killed by an army of ants."

Meghavarna inquired about this story. The old minister narrated the following tale:

The Snake and the Ants

A snake named Atidarp lived in a hole. He was enormous in size. One day, he tried to emerge from his hole using some other exit, which was too narrow. The snake was wounded and began to bleed. The smell of the blood reached some ants. They swarmed all over the snake and began to bite its wounds. This made the snake writhe in pain. Ultimately, the snake could not bear the pain and died.

Insight: Unity gave the ants a great conquest. Even man finds it difficult to destroy a snake. Being organised and united is the secret of the ants' success at all times. This is a great lesson for the common man and leaders to learn.

After narrating this story, the old minister Sthirjivi revealed his plan to kill the owl. He told Meghavarna: "Treat me as if I were your enemy. Put some blood on my body and push me down from the tree. I will try to find the place where the owl lives by winning the confidence of his detective. You and all the other crows must go to Rishimukh Mountain and live there for the time being. We will attack the owls during the daytime as soon as we discover their hideout."

Meghavarna followed his instructions. Both began a mock fight. Meghavarna daubed some blood on his body and pushed Sthirjivi down. Meghavarna then flew away to Rishimukh Mountain along with the other crows.

Krikalika – the detective of the owls – was watching all this. He went back to the king and informed him that the enemy king had fled along with the other crows.

The king owl thought this was the right time to attack as the enemy was scared. Not finding any crow on the tree, he ordered his attendants to find out where the crows had gone.

Acting as if he was severely wounded, Sthirjivi began making sounds to attract the owls. When the owls heard his voice, they came towards him in order to kill him. Sthirjivi requested them to arrange a meeting with their king as he had some very important information to divulge. The unsuspecting owls took him to their king, Arimardan.

Before Arimardan, Sthirjivi said: "My king Meghavarna wanted to attack you. I tried my best to stop him by saying that you were more powerful, so it would be better for him to seek your protection. He thought I was your spy and attacked me. I want to take revenge, so help me go to his place."

After hearing this, Arimardan consulted his ministers on what was to be done. A minister, Raktaksh, said it would be better to kill him, as the enemy was weak at the moment. If this was not done, he could emerge as a threat in the future.

"Once doubt erupts between friends, the friendship no longer remains the same, just like in the case of the Brahmin and a cobra."

Arimardan was curious to know this story. Raktaksh narrated this tale...

The Brahmin and the Cobra

O nce upon a time, in a village there lived a poor Brahmin called Hari Dutt. He owned a small piece of land that he cultivated for his livelihood. But it was not a very rewarding job and for most part of the year he led a hand-to-mouth existence.

One day, while resting under a tree in the middle of his field, the Brahmin saw a cobra with its hood raised as if ready to strike. Perhaps, Hari Dutt thought, he had to live in poverty because he was not worshipping the cobra.

He brought a bowl full of milk and offered it to the cobra. The cobra drank the milk and slipped back into his hole silently without harming the Brahmin. Next morning, when Hari Dutt went to his field, he was amazed to find a gold coin in the bowl. Now he started feeding the cobra with milk daily and everyday received a gold coin in return.

One day, the Brahmin had to visit another village to attend some urgent work. Before leaving, he instructed his son to feed the cobra with milk. The son kept the bowl full of milk near the mouth of the hole where the cobra lived.

The next morning, when he went to collect the bowl, he was surprised to find a gold coin in it. He thought there must be some treasure inside the cobra's hole. So he tried to kill the cobra after digging up the hole. But he only injured the cobra, which in turn bit him. The Brahmin's son died and was cremated in the same field by his neighbours.

Insight: The Brahmin should have realised that his son was too immature to be given the responsibility of feeding the cobra. Nor did he inform his son about the gold coin he would find. Poor judgement on the father's part, added to immaturity on the son's part, resulted in the disaster. When you delegate responsibility, always find the right person for the job and brief him carefully on all the details to avoid any untoward consequences.

When Hari Dutt returned, he heard the news of his son's death. But instead of feeling sorry for his son, he supported the cobra's action: "*A person not compassionate with people who have taken refuge with him is destroyed* in the same way that the swans living in Padmasarovar lost their habitat."

All the neighbours curiously asked about this story. Hari Dutt narrated the following tale:

The King and the Golden Swans

There lived a king named Chitrarath. There was a big lake in his palace that was well guarded. In the lake lived a flock of swans with golden wings. The king would get a golden wing from them every six months.

One day, a big bird that also had golden wings arrived at the lake. For fear of losing their value, the swans were not pleased by the arrival of the uninvited guest. They requested him to go back but the big bird refused. The swans told him: "This lake belongs to us because we pay tax for living here."

The big bird met the king and complained: "The swans are not permitting me to stay in the lake. They say they have purchased the lake from you and now even you cannot do anything to them."

The king was very angry. He ordered his men to kill the arrogant swans. An old swan saw the king's men coming. He realised what this meant. He advised all the other swans to fly away before the soldiers reached the lake.

Insight: While being hospitable has its rewards, being inhospitable has its consequences, which can sometimes be too high for the host. It is a good policy to be accommodating with your guests.

After completing his story, Hari Dutt went to the cobra with a bowl of milk. He wanted to please the cobra once again with his worship. Without emerging from his hole, the cobra said: "Your greed has so blinded you that you don't feel any pain or sorrow on your son's death. From now onwards, the friendship between us will never be the same as it used to be earlier. Neither can I forget the blows your son rained on me and nor will you forget your son's death. Each of us will be suspicious of the other from now on. So forget about the previous friendship; it can never be real."

The snake then presented Hari Dutt with a diamond for the last time and told him never to come again. The greedy Brahmin went away cursing his dead son.

Insight: If we wish to cultivate humane qualities, it is necessary to guard against greed or lust making us insensitive to pain and sorrow. If we lose our emotions, we run the risk of becoming ruthless. Once we reach this point, there can be no limits to greed, which turns our unsavoury behaviour into a vicious circle. Then, nothing will satisfy you; not even diamonds.

Completing his story, Raktaksh said: "You can rule without any obstacle only after the killing of Meghavarna."

Arimardan, the king of the owls, asked another minister, Kruraksha, for his opinion.

Kruraksha said *it was not proper for a king to kill a person who has taken refuge with him.* Then he narrated this story:

85

The Virtuous Pigeon and the Fowler

A fowler was once wandering in the forest in search of prey. He was so cruel that he had been expelled from his society.

One day he caught a female pigeon. Shutting her in a cage, the fowler again wandered in search of prey. Suddenly, dark clouds gathered in the sky and it began raining heavily. Afraid, the fowler began looking for shelter. He saw a big tree and took shelter under it.

When the rain stopped, he looked upward and said: "Please listen, whoever is living in this tree. I have taken refuge with you. I am suffering from hunger and cold. Please protect me."

A male pigeon living in this tree was wailing for his lost partner. The female pigeon recognised the tree and, looking upwards, was pleased to see her husband. She requested her husband to save the life of the hungry fowler, saying: "Do not be angry with the fowler because he has put me in this cage. I am just reaping the fruits of my past karma, you must do your duty and protect this hungry fowler."

The male pigeon then asked the fowler what he could do for him. The fowler said he was suffering from cold. The male pigeon brought a spark of fire and put it on some dry leaves. In a short while, a fire was ignited, which protected the fowler from the severe cold.

Now, realising there was no food to treat his guest, the male pigeon became very sad. He decided to give up his life by jumping into the burning fire, so that his guest could survive by eating his flesh. And he did so.

The fowler was very ashamed of himself. Releasing the female pigeon from his cage, he burnt the equipment that he used for trapping birds and decided to atone for his sins by leading an austere life.

The female pigeon could not tolerate her sorrow and jumped into the same fire. Seeing this, the fowler also sacrificed his life in the forest conflagration.

After finishing the story, Kruraksha said: "The life of a person who has sought refuge should be protected even at the cost of one's life."

Insight: Human beings have a lot to learn about hospitality towards guests and fidelity to their mates from this pair of pigeons. The basics of good hospitality require that you offer the best to your guest.

Arimardan then consulted his third minister, Deeptaksha. Deeptaksha was of the view that it was not worth killing Sthirjivi, saying: "Like the Brahmin, we can use his visit to our advantage."

Deeptaksha then narrated the following story:

The Old Merchant and His Young Wife

An old merchant named Kamatur lived in a city. One day his wife died. After some time, he married a young woman who was the daughter of a poor grocer, who gave a lot of wealth as dowry. His young wife was very unhappy with him and never expressed any love for him. Silently, she cursed her fate, but was unable to do anything.

One night when the old merchant and his young wife were sleeping, a burglar broke into their house. When the merchant's wife saw the burglar, she was terrified and hugged the old merchant tightly. The old merchant was surprised at this, as she had never shown any affection for him earlier. He began looking all around him and noticed the burglar. The old merchant was very happy that because of the burglar, his young wife had embraced him for the first time. He thought that if the burglar came daily, his young wife would embrace him every day. So he quietly requested the burglar: "Take whatever you wish, but please visit our home daily."

After completing his story, Deeptaksha said: "The merchant had considered the intruder as his benefactor, even though he was a petty thief. So what does one say about Sthirjivi, who has sought our refuge? We can use him to our benefit. So, according to me, Sthirjivi should not be killed."

Now Arimardan asked his fourth minister, Vakranas, his opinion. "Differences between enemy ranks are very beneficial for opponents. Because, in this way, a thief pardoned somebody's life and a demon saved the lives of two bullocks."

Arimardan asked about this story. Vakranas narrated the following tale:

The Thief and the Demon

There once lived a poor Brahmin named Drona, whose only means of livelihood was begging for alms. He had never seen the pleasures of life. His hair had grown long and so had his unshaved beard. His physique had become weak due to constant hardship under harsh weather conditions.

Taking pity on him, one day someone presented Drona with a pair of calves, along with a large quantity of grains and cereals. Since then, he looked after the calves with great care. With time, the calves grew into robust oxen.

Soon, the oxen began to attract covetous eyes. A thief decided to steal them. As the thief ventured towards the Brahmin's house, he met a demon on the way and was terrified. The thief asked him who he was and where he was going. The demon replied he was going to devour the Brahmin. The thief revealed he was going to steal the Brahmin's oxen. Both then went to the Brahmin's house together.

The Brahmin was sleeping at this time. The demon wanted to devour the Brahmin first, but the thief wished to do his job before that. Both began quarrelling on this count. Hearing the commotion, the Brahmin woke up. He drove the demon away by chanting sacred mantras and beat the thief with a stick.

Having completed his story, Vakranas said: "This is why I say that *differences in the enemy's ranks are always advantageous.*"

Insight: Competition among business people should give you ideas to capitalise on the situation and capture the market. On the other hand, if you need to fight an enemy, join hands with other enemies of that person. As is widely known, the enemy of an enemy is a friend. There is strength in unity.

Arimardan then asked the fifth minister, Prakarkarna, his opinion.

Prakarkarna said: "Sthirjivi is unworthy of being killed. Perhaps by sparing his life we would be able to lead our lives peacefully. It is said that those who do not protect the secrets of each other are destroyed just like the snakes who destroyed each other by revealing their secrets."

Arimardan asked: "How did this happen?"

Prakarkarna narrated the following story:

Tale of the Two Snakes

There lived a king named Devashakti. One day, a snake entered his son's stomach through his open mouth while he was sleeping. This made the prince very weak day by day. The king consulted many physicians, in vain. This dejected the prince so much, he began living in a hermitage after renouncing everything. There was another king named Bali. He had two daughters. One of them would greet the king daily in the morning saying: "Long live the king! By whose grace we get all kinds of joy and pleasure."

But the other princess greeted him saying: "O king! Taste the fruits of your actions."

One day, he became so angry with his second daughter that he decided to marry her to a stranger as a punishment. He told his minister: "Give this wicked girl to some alien, so that she herself tastes the fruits of her actions."

So the second princess was given to the prince who had a snake in his stomach and was living in the hermitage. The princess accepted him as her husband without complaining. She once took him to another city. There, she requested him to wait till she returned after making arrangements for lunch. The prince waited at the edge of a lake, where a pleasant breeze made him drowsy and he soon fell asleep. The snake living in the stomach was now gasping for air. So it emerged from the open mouth of the prince. Right there on the ground, another snake was basking after emerging from his hole. Both the snakes began talking to each other.

In the meantime, the princess had arrived. She was amazed to see snakes that talked. Hiding behind a tree, she eavesdropped on their conversation. The second snake was telling the first one: "O wicked fellow! Why are you tormenting this prince? Why don't you quit living in his stomach?"

The first snake replied: "Why are you polluting the treasure contained in the two pots which lie beneath your hole?"

The second snake angrily retorted: "Doesn't anybody know you could be killed easily if the prince is made to drink old and boiled kanji (rice starch) mixed with mustard seeds?"

The first snake replied in anger: "Doesn't anybody know that you can be killed by pouring boiling oil or boiling water into your hole."

When the princess heard this, she did exactly what the snakes had prescribed and both were killed. The prince was cured. Besides, he had secured a good wife and a lot of treasure because of her wisdom. He returned to his father along with the princess and newly-found wealth. There they lived happily.

If secrets are revealed, it brings death and destruction. When Prakarkarna finished his story, he found Arimardan nodding his head in agreement.

But Raktaksha did not like this decision and said: "A country where wicked people are honoured and compassionate people dishonoured faces the danger of famine, death and fear."

But nobody listened to him. Sthirjivi was brought to the owls' hiding place.

Sthirjivi was pleased that his plan was working successfully. He said: "I am of no use to you in this injured condition. Throw me into the fire, so that I may die. In my next birth, I wish to be reborn as an owl to take my revenge against the wicked Meghavarna."

Raktaksha said: "Dear! You are not only wicked and mean, but also an expert in mocking. But listen! Your nature is not going to change even if you take birth as an owl."

Then Raktaksha narrated the following story to prove his point:

The Hermit and the Mouse

There once lived a hermit named Shalankayan. One day he saw a small mouse being carried away by a hawk. At that time he was going towards the Ganges to bathe. Taking pity on the mouse, he rescued it from the talons of the hawk.

He then brought the small mouse to his hermitage. Through his spiritual powers, the hermit transformed the mouse into a beautiful girl.

When the girl grew up, the hermit looked for a suitable groom. He thought the Sun would be an ideal match for her. He invoked the Sun with mantras. When the Sun appeared, he asked the girl: "Are you interested in marrying the Sun, who illuminates the whole world?"

The girl was reluctant. She said the Sun would be too hot for her to bear. And the Sun said that the cloud would be an ideal match for her... "because he is more powerful than me".

The hermit then invoked the Cloud. The girl again expressed her reluctance, saying the Cloud was like a vagabond. The Cloud said the Mountain was more powerful than him. The hermit invoked the Mountain, but the girl refused to marry him saying the Mountain was too heavy and she would be crushed under his weight. The Mountain

said the mouse was more powerful than himself... "because he is capable of digging up holes even through me".

The hermit then called a mouse. When the girl was asked about her opinion, she happily agreed to marry the mouse. The hermit transformed her into a small mouse and married her to the mouse.

Completing his story, Raktaksha said: *"The nature of a man always remains unchanged."*

Insight: It is difficult for us to master our nature, hence it is not possible to change it. It is best for man to use his rationality to develop both the right values as well as the emotional intelligence needed to exercise enough self-control to live according to these beliefs and values, instead of a life of pretence.

But Arimardan did not pay any heed and Sthirjivi was taken to their cave with full honours. Arimardan instructed his attendants that Sthirjivi should be given a place of his liking. Sthirjivi thought it would be better for him to stay outside, as it would help him execute his plans without being noticed by anybody.

He told Arimardan: "O Lord! Even though I am your well-wisher, the fact remains that I belong to an enemy camp. So it would not be proper for you to allow me to live inside your cave. I would consider myself fortunate if I am allowed to stay at the door of your cave."

Arimardan agreed and Sthirjivi was given a variety of dishes to eat. Within a few days, he became fat.

Raktaksha did not like this. He told the ministers: "All of you, including the king, are fools. It has rightly been said that first of all I am a fool, secondly, the fowler is a fool too, then the king and the ministers are fools. All of us belong to the same bunch of fools."

All the owls were very surprised but did not understand anything. They asked him to elaborate. Raktaksha then narrated the following story:

The Bird With Golden Droppings

A bird named Sindhuk lived in the forest at the foothills of a mountain. Its droppings had the unique quality of getting transformed into gold as soon as they touched the ground.

One day a fowler saw this strange incident and trapped the bird in his net and brought it to his home. At home, the fowler put the bird in a cage.

Though the fowler was happy he would get gold every day, he was also worried that once the king heard about this miraculous bird, he would not only lose the bird but might also be hanged. So he decided to present the bird to the king. He went to the king and told him about the bird's unique quality.

The king was happy. He instructed his minister to see that the bird was kept with great care. But the minister said: "O King! It is not proper to cage this bird. I do not believe this fowler. The bird should be set free."

The king instructed that the bird be set free. The bird then flew away and sat on the main gate of the palace and said: "First of all I was a fool, secondly, the fowler was a fool, thirdly, the king was a fool and fourthly, the ministers were fools."

Saying this the bird flew away.

Insight: One must not easily believe others without using one's own judgement. There is nothing to be gained by acting on hearsay and nothing lost if we check the facts before acting on what we hear from others. By blindly believing others, you may realise too late that your life has turned into a comedy of errors and you have been living in a fool's paradise.

After Raktaksha finished his story, Arimardan was still unconvinced. Raktaksha then decided to go to some other cave along with his well-wishers, saying: "*A person who does not think about and solve his most serious problems is sure to regret it later on.* I have passed my whole life in this forest and have now grown old but never in my life have I heard a cave talking."

All the owls asked about the story of a cave that talked.

Raktaksha narrated the following tale:

The Jackal and the Lion

A lion named Kharankhar lived in a forest. One day, when he did not find any prey and was driven by hunger, he entered a cave thinking: 'There must be some animal living in this cave.' He waited inside the cave patiently for the arrival of a potential meal.

The cave belonged to a jackal named Dadhipuchchh. When the jackal returned and was about to enter the cave, he noticed the footprints of the lion leading into the cave. However, there were no footprints coming out of the cave.

The jackal realised that the lion was still inside the cave awaiting his arrival. To confirm his suspicion he employed a trick. He shouted: "O Cave! O Cave!" Then he paused for a while and said: "Why don't you call me back. Don't you know that I do not enter you unless you invite me?"

The lion heard all this and thought that the cave must be responding to the jackal's call every time. 'Perhaps his cave is scared of me and that's why it is not responding to the jackal's call,' thought the lion.

The lion decided to respond to the jackal's call, imitating the cave. He called out: "Come in! Come in!"

When the jackal heard the lion's roar, he understood everything and ran away.

Insight: Only patience and hard work may not be sufficient to satisfy our needs – we must use our brains also. The jackal beat the king of the forest with his brains and the king had to put up with his hunger. The higher up you are in the hierarchy, the more you will have to utilise brain power, else you may be left hungry nursing your ambitions, much like the lion.

After completing his story, Raktaksha shifted to another place along with his family and well-wishers.

Sthirjivi was happy that a major obstacle in his path had been removed. He then started collecting wood in his nest. The foolish owls did not realise the purpose behind his action. After some days, a large pile of wood was collected.

One day, at sunrise when the owls were unable to see, Sthirjivi went to call Meghavarna, who was living at Rishimukh Mountain. When he reached there, he told Meghavarna: "Lord! Be quick! I have stored a huge pile of wood at the door of the owls' cave. Now we must ignite that pile before the detective owls come to know about our plan."

Meghavarna then fetched a piece of burning wood and holding it in his beak, he placed it amongst the pile of wood. The fire spread rapidly and all the owls were soon charred to death. As he lay dying, Arimardan realised that had he listened to Raktaksha, they would not have met such a sad and fiery end.

Meghavarna then returned to his previous abode along with the other crows. Meghavarna was curious to know about Sthirjivi's plan that had enabled him to accomplish his mission successfully.

Insight: Sweet talk from the enemy should not blind us to reality and impair our logic and thinking. Why would the enemy become a friend suddenly? Have you given him a strong enough reason for this change of heart? We need to weigh all these points before consorting with the enemy.

When Sthirjivi had narrated the whole story, he said: *"When the situation demands, an intelligent person should be prepared to even carry the enemy on his shoulders, just as the snake who had devoured thousands of frogs after carrying each of them on his hood did."*

Meghavarna curiously asked about the story.

Sthirjivi narrated the following tale:

The Frogs and the Snake

There once lived an old snake named Mandavish. Because of old age he faced serious difficulties in finding prey. At last, he devised a plan. Arriving at the shores of a nearby lake, he sat there like an ascetic. A frog saw him and curiously asked why he was not making any effort to acquire food.

The snake replied deceitfully: "How can an unfortunate person like me have a desire to eat? Last night I tried to catch a frog, but it managed to slip away and hid among the Brahmins, who were taking their bath. I mistook the thumb of a Brahmin's son for the frog and bit him. The boy died. The Brahmin cursed me into becoming a vehicle for the frogs, so that only through their blessings could I get my food. Therefore, I have come here to become your vehicle."

The frog went back into the lake and informed his king, Jalpaad and all the other frogs. Jalpaad believed the story and emerged from the lake to have a ride on the back of the snake.

The snake pleased Jalpaad with his asceticism and took him for a ride on his hood. Jalpaad thoroughly enjoyed his ride. Soon it became his daily routine. After some days, the snake was creeping slowly but it was all part of his plan. Jalpaad asked about the reason for his slow movement. Mandavish replied that as he had not eaten anything for the past many days, he was feeling very hungry.

The foolish Jalpaad instructed him to devour some small frogs. Mandavish was very pleased but did not show his happiness. In this way, Mandavish killed and ate many frogs. The foolish Jalpaad did not realise that he was instrumental in the killing of his own people by granting Mandavish permission to eat "some small frogs". In the end, Mandavish devoured Jalpaad too.

Insight: Besides displaying foolish belief in the words of an enemy in disguise, the king of the frogs put himself in deeper trouble by his extreme insensitivity towards his own kind, allowing the snake to kill them. If a leader has no concern for people of his own kind, why would another group have any concern for them? Lack of concern for the welfare of those under you could lead everyone to doom.

After completing his story, Sthirjivi told Meghavarna that he too had killed his enemies just like Mandavish. He said: *"A mean person does not even dare to undertake a task for fear of potential obstacles. A mediocre person does undertake a task but quits midway when faced with obstacles. The outstanding person, however, accomplishes his task once he undertakes it, despite obstacles."*

Sthirjivi then requested Meghavarna to rule fearlessly as all hurdles in his path had been removed and all enemies slain. "I want to take rest now as I have grown old," said Sthirjivi. *Sthirjivi also advised Meghavarna not to get discouraged by adversities, as it was natural to face some kind of obstacles in life.* "Even Sri Rama could not lead an obstacle-free life."

Sthirjivi cited many examples from the life of great men like the Pandavas and the destruction of Ravana to prove his point. Thus, having advised Meghavarna to rule justly, Sthirjivi retired.

The Fourth Tantra – Labdhapranasha ___

The Monkey and the Crocodile

A *person who has patience and an unwavering mind even during an emergency can easily overcome any crisis,* as was the case with the monkey.

There was a big jamun tree along the shore of a lake laden with fruit throughout the year. On the tree lived a monkey named Raktamukh. The big, delicious fruits were enough to sustain the monkey. One day, a crocodile emerged from the lake and sat under the tree. The monkey treated the crocodile well and gave him some jamuns to eat.

The crocodile had never tasted such sweet fruits in his life. After chatting with the monkey for some time, the crocodile returned to the lake.

Since that day the crocodile came ashore daily and the monkey gave him sweet jamuns to eat. Very soon, the crocodile and the monkey became good friends. One day the monkey gave some jamuns for the crocodile's wife also. His wife relished the sweet taste of the fruit. So every day when the crocodile returned home, he took some fruit for his wife also.

One day the crocodile's wife said: "Dear! The heart of the monkey who eats these sweet fruits daily would be so sweet. I want to eat his heart."

The crocodile tried hard to convince her that it was impossible for him to bring the heart of the monkey, as he was his fast friend, "...so I cannot kill him".

His wife jealously retorted: "I know very well whom you go to meet. It is not the monkey but some other female crocodile who is prettier than me and with whom you pass the whole day flirting."

The crocodile's wife began making all kinds of allegations and threatened to end her life. The ruckus caused great worry to the crocodile.

That day, he reached the shore very late. The monkey was awaiting his friend eagerly. When the crocodile approached, the monkey asked him why he was so late.

The crocodile replied: "My wife wants to meet you, my friend. She says I am so selfish that although you give me sweet jamuns to eat daily, I have not treated you even once. So she has invited you for dinner and has already made all the preparations."

The monkey happily accepted the invitation, but asked: "How will I reach your residence, which is deep under the sea?"

The crocodile replied that reaching his residence was not a problem, because it was on a small island and not under the sea.

So the monkey happily jumped down the tree and rode on the back of the crocodile. The crocodile proceeded towards his home carrying the monkey on his back. After swimming for a while, the crocodile revealed his real intention, saying: "I am taking you to my home so that my wife can eat your sweet and delicious heart."

The clever monkey quickly sized up the entire situation and said: "Friend! Why did you not tell me this earlier? I would have brought my heart along, which is kept on the tree."

The crocodile looked on in amazement and was quite confused. The monkey requested him to return to the shore so that he could fetch his heart. The stupid crocodile failed to understand the trick and swam back to the shore. As soon as he reached the shore, the monkey swiftly bounded up the tree.

When the crocodile saw that the monkey was still on the tree, he requested him to come down immediately with his heart, as it was getting late.

The monkey replied: "Just go away and never come back you fool! You have breached my trust. You are a traitor. Have you ever heard of anybody having two hearts?"

Insight 1: Beware of the evil intentions of your rivals or competitors. The monkey was lucky that the crocodile happened to be a fool. You may not be so lucky.

Insight 2: Strong emotional ties can cloud our objectivity. Despite not wanting to betray a friend, many do so at the request of a spouse or a member of the opposite sex. Such mistakes can ruin your reputation. When the attachment is very close, we have to be more careful as the loved one may resort to emotional blackmail. If this happens, we need to resist this person, rather than give in to manipulative behaviour, which will shame us. For this reason, it is unwise to develop intimate relations with people at the workplace.

Dumbstruck, the crocodile softly cursed his foolishness. He then tried to convince the monkey that he was just joking and his wife never wanted to eat his heart. But the monkey admonished him saying: "Just go away! *A starving man can go to any extent. A poor man is devoid of compassion.* Gentleman, go and tell Priyadarshan that Gangadutt does not visit this well again."

The crocodile did not comprehend anything and asked the monkey what he was talking about. The monkey narrated the following story:

The Snake and the Foolish Frog

A frog named Gangadutt lived in a well. For some reason, he had developed hostility towards his relatives living in the same well. Having been tormented by them, he somehow managed to escape from the well with the help of pulleys once used to draw water from the well. He wanted to take revenge on the other frogs. Suddenly, he saw a black cobra entering his hole. He decided to seek the cobra's help for this purpose.

Standing at the mouth of the hole, he called out to the snake and explained his ordeal. The snake agreed to go with him. Both of them managed to enter the well with the help of the pulley.

The frog showed a hole in the wall of the well to the snake for concealment. The snake began to live in the hole and devoured all the frogs one by one. Gangadutt was pleased to see that his revenge was working well. When the snake had eaten all his enemies, he requested Gangadutt to provide him with some more frogs. The snake threatened that he would start killing Gangadutt's family members if he did not heed his request.

Gangadutt realised he had committed a blunder by taking the snake's help. The very next day the snake devoured Gangadutt's son. Gangadutt wailed in grief. He warned his wife that both of them would meet the same fate unless they escaped from the well. His fear came true as the very next day it was the turn of his wife. Now Gangadutt alone survived.

One day the hungry snake asked Gangadutt to provide more frogs. Gangadutt replied: "If you allow me to go out of this well I can bring many frogs for you."

The snake allowed him to go out on the promise that Gangadutt would return soon. Gangadutt went out of the well with the help of the pulley.

When Gangadutt did not return for many days the snake was worried. He asked a chameleon living in the well to find out the whereabouts of Gangadutt: "You are a close friend of Gangadutt. Just tell him that I will not devour him if he comes back."

The chameleon met Gangadutt and told him that his friend was awaiting him. Gangadutt replied: "Go and tell him I will not return."

Insight: Revenge can backfire. Think of the pros and cons before taking revenge – this may help you relinquish the idea of revenge. We often pay a heavy price for our mistakes. It is important to find the means to minimise our mistakes or to ensure that the price we pay will not be overwhelming, and also see that we don't repeat the mistakes we made in the first place.

After completing his story, the monkey told the crocodile that he too would not go to his home, just like Gangadutt. The crocodile told the monkey that if he did not go to his home, he would end his life.

The monkey replied: "O wicked crocodile! Do you think I am a fool like that donkey Lambakarna?"

Observation: The crocodile tries blackmail but the monkey resists.

The crocodile asked about Lambakarna's story. The monkey narrated the following tale:

Lambakarna – the Donkey

A lion named Karalkeshar once lived in a forest. The lion had a jackal named Dhusarak as his attendant who followed him like a shadow. Every day, the lion would hunt an animal and after having his share he left the remaining meat for the jackal. Thus the jackal also passed his time happily.

One day, the lion had a fight with an elephant and was seriously injured. Because of his master's injury, the jackal too could not get anything to eat and began to starve.

A few days later, the jackal told the lion: "Lord! Prolonged starvation has made me weak. I am now unable to even walk a few steps. In such a condition, how can I serve you?"

The lion instructed the jackal to find any animal that he could kill despite his injuries.

The jackal then went towards the village in search of an animal.

At the outskirts of the village, he saw a very lean donkey grazing there. The donkey's name was Lambakarna. The jackal asked him: "Uncle! How are you? How thin and weak you have become? Is everything going well?"

The donkey replied: "Oh no! Nothing is going well! My master only extracts hard work from me but does not feed me properly. This is why I have become so weak."

The cunning jackal said: "If this is so, come along with me. I know a place that is full of green grass. In a very short time you will grow very healthy."

But the donkey had some apprehensions: "I am a domestic animal. I fear that the wild animals will not like my presence in the forest and could even kill me."

The jackal assured him his apprehensions were baseless as the area was well protected by him. But the donkey remained unconvinced.

The jackal then thought of a plan to lure the donkey: "O uncle! You must come along with me without fear. You will be pleased to know that three female donkeys are already in that area, enjoying their lives grazing peacefully on the green grass the whole day. They are interested in getting married and have requested me to bring a donkey so that they can marry."

This temptation was too much for the donkey and he agreed to go along with the jackal. The jackal reached the forest accompanied by the donkey. The lion was very pleased on seeing the donkey and tried to get up. As soon as the donkey saw the lion getting up he tried to flee. The lion attacked the fleeing donkey, but the latter managed to escape.

Angry with the lion, the jackal said: "You are not even capable of killing a donkey, how could you fight an elephant?"

The lion felt very ashamed. The jackal then said that he would try to lure the donkey a second time. "This time you must be careful," warned the jackal.

Though the lion was not so sure of the donkey's repeat arrival, he still agreed to remain alert. The jackal then followed the donkey's tracks.

103

Some time later, he saw the donkey standing beside a lake and said: "Uncle! Why did you run away?"

The donkey replied: "Son! I was almost killed! Who was the animal that attacked me?"

The cunning jackal replied: "O uncle! That was one of the three female donkeys. She took such a fancy to you that she tried to embrace you immediately, but you did not realise she was expressing her love and ran away like a coward. She cannot live without you now and has vowed to end her life, if she does not secure you as her husband. You must marry her."

The foolish donkey believed the cunning jackal and returned to the lion. But this time the lion did not make a mistake and killed the stupid donkey.

After killing the donkey, the lion went to have a bath, instructing the jackal to guard the dead donkey. As soon as the lion was out of sight, the jackal ate the ears and heart of the donkey.

When the lion returned, he found the ears and heart missing. He was very angry and suspected this was the doing of the cunning jackal. But the jackal fibbed that the donkey did not have ears and a heart from birth: "If he had had ears, would he not have been able to hear your roar. Similarly, if he had a heart he would not have returned even after having been attacked by you."

The lion was convinced by this explanation.

Insight: When people try repeatedly to convince you of something, they usually have their own interest rather than yours in mind. Beware! They can convince you even after duping people you know. The donkey did not learn a lesson from the first bad experience and paid with his life the second time round. Let's not be donkeys and give deceitful jackals a second chance after they have duped us once.

Concluding his story, the monkey told the crocodile that not only was he an impostor, he was also a fool who failed because he revealed the truth. "If a foolish impostor reveals his plan by telling the truth, he fails in his plan just like Yudhisthir the potter."

The crocodile curiously asked about the story of Yudhisthir. The monkey narrated the following tale:

104

Yudhisthir — the Potter

There once lived a potter named Yudhisthir. One day, he drank to his heart's content, fell down intoxicated and injured his head. In the absence of proper treatment, his wound subsequently grew sore. However, when the wound healed ultimately, it left a gaping scar on Yudhisthir's forehead.

One year, due to failure of the rains, a severe famine gripped the entire city. Along with his friends, Yudhisthir migrated to another city. When the king of that city saw a mark on his head, he thought that Yudhisthir might have acquired it in battle and inducted Yudhisthir into his army. Considering him a brave soldier, the king instructed his generals to take special care of him.

One day, the king was attacked by an enemy. While distributing weapons to his soldiers, he asked Yudhisthir: "O brave man! In which battle did you get this injury? Which caste do you belong to?"

Foolish Yudhisthir revealed the truth: "O King! I am a potter and got this injury under the influence of an intoxicant."

The king was ashamed of having inducted Yudhisthir into his army without scrutinising his past. He ordered his men to kick Yudhisthir out of the palace. Yudhisthir requested the king to test his bravery in the battlefield.

The king replied: "It does not matter even if you are brave, the fact is people like you are incapable of killing elephants."

Insight: Some secrets should never be revealed. They embarrass others and to overcome their embarrassment they will treat you like an impostor and victimise you. If you want others to treat you with respect, think twice before telling them any personal details that in their narrow-mindedness they may hold against you.

Yudhisthir was astonished how bravery could be equated with one's status. The king narrated the following story to prove his point:

The Lion and the Jackal's Pup

A lion and a lioness lived in a forest. Once, the lioness gave birth to two cubs. The lion brought meat for the cubs by hunting animals. One day the lion did not find any prey. In the evening, while returning to his den, he found a jackal's pup.

He brought the young jackal to the lioness and said: "This is what I have got today. Have some light refreshment. Tomorrow, I will certainly make arrangements for a heavy meal. I did not kill this pup myself because of his tender age."

The lioness too felt sorry for the pup, refrained from killing him and fed him her milk. The lion and the lioness treated the jackal pup very well. Besides, the cubs and the pup played together.

One day, while the three of them were playing, they saw an elephant. The cubs prepared to attack the elephant, but the jackal pup thought: "This elephant is my enemy. If I do not run away, I will be killed."

Thinking thus, he ran away. When the cubs saw him running away, they too followed suit.

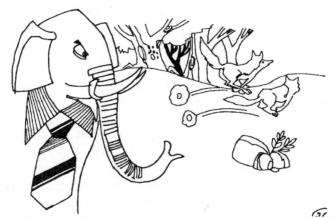

It has rightly been said: "During a battle, *if even one soldier loses courage it affects the morale of the entire army. Similarly, one valiant soldier can boost the morale of all soldiers.*"

Insight: Your background does matter. In real life too, the son of a jackal may not have the same courage as the son of a lion. Nor are they likely to have been brought up in the same manner. As a leader, it is important to know that one member's qualities can inspire the whole team to perform. Similarly, a single member who underperforms can demoralise the whole team. So a group of go-getters do well together rather than a mixed group.

When the cubs narrated the story of how the jackal pup had fled on seeing an elephant, the lion was very angry. Fearing that the angry lion might kill him, the lioness told the jackal pup: "Son! The species to which you belong cannot kill elephants. I have full sympathy with you, but the lion is very angry and he may not spare your life. So run away if you want to save your life."

Hearing this, the horrified jackal pup ran away.

Completing his story, the king told Yudhisthir to run away, else he would be killed by other warriors once they knew his real identity.

Insight: Uncontrollable and unreasonable anger can be compared to insanity. Keep away from it or the consequences may be tragic. Secondly, to fit into a group one must have something in common — otherwise one would be the odd man out and get into trouble sooner or later.

The monkey said: "A man can go to any extent to please his wife. For example, he can tonsure his head on forbidden days like Ashtami, Chaudas etc. or he can even neigh like a horse."

The crocodile did not understand anything and asked: "What do you mean?"

The monkey narrated the following tale:

Mand and Varruchi

A great king named Mand once ruled a country. He had a very able minister, Varruchi, who was a great scholar. One day, for some reason, Varruchi's wife was angry with him. He tried his best but could not placate his wife and asked: "Dear! What should I do to please you? I can do anything to see you smiling."

His wife angrily replied: "I will be pleased only when you bow before me with a tonsured head."

Varruchi did as asked and his wife felt very happy and forgot all about her anger.

Similarly, for some unknown reason, Mand's wife once became angry with him. The king tried his best to placate her, but the queen was unmoved. At last, the king asked: "Dear Queen! What should I do to make you happy? I can do anything for your happiness."

The queen replied: "I will be happy only when I sit on your back, just like a rider on horseback. You will also have to neigh like a horse."

The king had no choice but to obey. He did as the queen asked and she was pleased.

The next morning when Varruchi arrived with his tonsured head, the king made a joke of it and asked about the occasion for which he had tonsured his head.

Varruchi replied: "What does a man not give his wife on her demands? He neighs and walks on all fours just like a horse and can even get his head tonsured on an auspicious day like Ashtami."

The sheepish king realised that Varruchi knew how he had acceded to the queen's unnatural request and kept mum with embarrassment.

Insight: You have to determine to what extent you can be influenced by others and the price you are willing to pay for it. To tonsure your head or neigh like a horse will be a humiliating experience, all the more so if others hear this, making it difficult for you to hold your head high in august company.

After completing the story, the monkey told the crocodile: "O wicked crocodile! You too are under the evil influence of your wife and can go to any extent to please her just like Mand and Varruchi. It was my good fortune that I was able to save my life. Had you not spoken the truth I would have been killed just like the donkey who was killed when he brayed and revealed his identity."

The crocodile was curious and asked about this story. The monkey then narrated the following tale:

Donkey in the Tiger's Skin

There once lived a poor washer, who had a donkey he was unable to feed properly. The donkey was very weak and gaunt because he did not get enough green grass to eat.

One day, while wandering in the forest, the washer saw a dead tiger. He at once skinned it and took the skin home. He thought that if he covered his donkey with the tiger's skin, it would have no problem while grazing in others' fields, as nobody would dare approach it. For many months, the clever scheme worked well and the donkey gained sound health and strength.

However, a few months later when the donkey was grazing in a field, he heard a female donkey braying in search of a mate. Immediately, the donkey began braying too. When the villagers heard the braying, they gathered in the field and killed the donkey.

Insight: Pretence is no good as a long-term strategy. If you fake abilities, sooner or later you will be exposed.

The monkey completed his story. The crocodile, however, continued to hang around. This angered the monkey, who said: "O wicked one! Why are you still waiting here? Will you go only after being disgraced like Shyamalak?"

The crocodile inquired about Shyamalak's story.

The monkey narrated the following tale:

Shyamalak – the Honoured Guest

There once lived a rich businessman named Ishwar. One day, four of his sons-in-law arrived from Ujjain. Ishwar treated them with great respect and honour, although they stayed with him for six months.

Ishwar then told his wife: "Dear! They are not thinking of returning because of our hospitality and the full respect they are receiving."

His wife replied: "I think they won't think of going back unless shown some disrespect."

Ishwar then advised his wife not to give them water to wash their feet. Ishwar's wife followed the instruction the next day. One of the sons-in-law named Garg was intelligent. He understood the subtle message and returned home.

The next day, the three remaining guests were given a small seat to sit upon. The second son-in-law, Soma, also departed.

The third day, the third son-in-law, Dutt, left for home after being given stale food.

But the fourth son-in-law, Shyamalak, stayed put. At last he too was forcibly shown the door.

Insight 1: Everyone's grasping power is not the same. Each one has to be taught in a manner commensurate with his capabilities. In other words, the cure has to match the intensity of the disease.

Insight 2: Do not burden others with unwanted company. Use common sense to discover if you are wanted by your peers or at a place of work. This is also true in the hospitality context. Never abuse a welcome by overstaying. The moral of the story holds good for relationships too, in and outside the home. If you don't take subtle hints that you are no longer welcome, the other person will be forced to ask you to leave more bluntly, which would be humiliating.

The monkey and the crocodile were so engrossed in their conversation that they failed to notice how much time had elapsed. Just then, another crocodile arrived and informed them that an intruder had captured the crocodile's home and his wife.

The crocodile requested the monkey to help him. Initially, the monkey was not interested in helping the crocodile, but could not refuse his repeated requests.

The monkey advised the crocodile to fight with the crocodile who had captured his home, saying: *"The superior man should be controlled by courtesy and humbleness; the powerful man should be brought under control by causing differences in his ranks. The mean man should be controlled through bribery and a well-matched opponent should be overpowered through battle."*

The crocodile requested the monkey to elaborate.

The monkey narrated the following tale:

Mahachaturak – the Jackal

A jackal named Mahachaturak once lived in a forest. One day he found a dead elephant. Although he tried his best, he could not eat even a small portion of the flesh because the elephant's hide was very thick and hard.

Right then a lion arrived there. The cunning jackal bowed in respect and said: "O Lord! You have arrived at the right time. I have been protecting this elephant for you. Please relish its flesh."

The lion replied that he did not eat prey killed by others and walked away. The jackal was happy that the lion had gone without eating the elephant.

Suddenly, a tiger arrived. The jackal shouted loudly: "O uncle! Why have you come here? This elephant has been killed by the lion, who has gone to take bath after instructing me to guard the kill. He has also asked me to inform him as soon as I see any tiger. He is very angry with tigers as a tiger once stole an elephant killed by him. So please go away as quickly as possible."

The tiger requested the jackal not to inform the lion about his presence and slunk away.

After the tiger's departure, a leopard arrived. The jackal welcomed him: "Welcome! Be my guest! You have arrived at lunchtime but how helpless I am. I cannot even provide you with something to eat. This elephant was killed by a lion, who has gone for his bath, instructing me to guard the kill till he returns. If I do not treat my guest, however, I will be committing a grave sin. So, you can relish the elephant while I stand guard. As soon as I see the lion coming, I will inform you."

The leopard agreed and began tearing the elephant's hide with his razor-sharp canines. The jackal watched him from a distance. When

111

the jackal saw that the leopard had torn enough of the hide for him to consume the flesh, the jackal came rushing towards the leopard: "O uncle! The lion is coming! Run! Run!"

The leopard fled. Since the tough hide of the elephant had now been penetrated, the jackal happily began to tuck into the elephant's flesh.

Right then another jackal arrived. The first jackal fought the second jackal bravely and killed him. He then enjoyed the flesh of the elephant for many days.

Insight: Presence of mind and courage are an unbeatable combination. And if you can pull off some harmless tricks to gain the upper hand, the mixture is fantastic! The tactics you employ to fight different competitors have to be varied, depending upon the strength of the person.

Finishing this story, the monkey advised the crocodile to fight the intruding crocodile who had captured his home. The monkey said: "Though it is easy to discover a means of livelihood in some foreign land, there is one hurdle – people of one's own caste become enemies."

The crocodile asked how it was possible for people from the same caste becoming enemies in a foreign land. The monkey narrated the following tale:

Chitrang – the Dog

A dog named Chitrang once lived in a city. Due to famine on one occasion, people began migrating en mass. Chitrang too decided to abandon that city and migrate to another city.

In the new environment, the dog found no difficulty in securing food as housewives in that city were very careless. The dog would enter a house and eat the food kept in the kitchen. Before long, he grew very fat.

Though he did not have any problem in procuring food, the other dogs of that city tormented him very much and even bit him. So one day he decided to return to his home city, thinking: "Even if I get little food, I will at least be safe in my own city."

When he returned home, friends enquired about life in the alien city.

Chitrang replied: *"Though food was easily available, life was not safe and secure."*

Insight 1: If you plan to emigrate, be prepared to face increased competition (and jealousy too) even from your own countrymen.

Insight 2: The story throws light on another aspect of one's nature dealing with needs and wants – when faced with famine and scarcity, the only thing we can think of is getting enough to eat. But the moment this need is met, we realise that other things in life are also important... Likewise, professionally, a good salary is not all that people look for – though it may be the most important factor – working conditions, stability and perks also matter.

Insight 3: The same principle is applicable to industry. In the initial stage, one dreams of simply growing. This achieved, one then wants to equal others. Next, one wants to be the best. Finally, once at the top, one desires to vanquish all competition... In essence, it is good, even healthy, to reach a stage when just a good fill is not sufficient and one wants more to be happy. However, it is essential to have a healthy ceiling for one's desires.

After hearing this story, the crocodile went to fight the intruding crocodile who had seized his residence. He drove the intruder out of his home and killed him. He then lived happily.

The Fifth Tantra — Aparikshitakaraka ___

The fifth tantra begins with the following shloka: KUDROSHTAM KUPARIGYATAM KUSHRUTAM KUPARIKSHITAM TANNAREN NA KARTAVYAM NAPITENATRA YAT KRITAM ||

Meaning: A man must never make the same mistake as the barber, who tried to accomplish his task without properly looking into its advantages and disadvantages, and without properly examining the consequences of his action.

In the city of Pataliputra lived a businessman named Manibhadra. Once a very rich man, he subsequently lost all his wealth because of his excessive involvement in religious and spiritual activities. He then began worrying about his poverty.

One day he decided to end his life by starving to death. The first day passed without much ado. When night came, however, he went to sleep and had a dream in which Padmanidhi said: "I am the wealth accumulated by your ancestors. Tomorrow morning I will come to your home in the same guise you are seeing me in right now. If you hit me with a stick on my head, I will transform myself into gold."

Manibhadra woke up from his sleep. He thought that perhaps he had such a dream because he worried about acquiring wealth all the time. In the morning his wife called a barber to have Manibhadra's head tonsured. Just as the barber arrived, a Jain monk arrived too. Manibhadra recognised him immediately and hit the monk on his head with a stick. The monk collapsed and was transformed into gold.

Manibhadra presented the barber with lots of gifts and requested him not to reveal the incident to anybody. The barber returned home happily.

Now the barber also wanted to acquire gold, so he went to a temple and invited some of the Jain monks to visit his house. When the monks arrived, the barber began hitting them on their heads with a stick. Some died on the spot, while the others were severely injured. The injured monks began crying for help. A soldier heard their cries and rushed to the spot. Taking stock of the situation, he took the barber into custody. Soon thereafter, the entire matter was taken to court.

When the judge asked the barber why he had killed the Jain monks, the barber narrated the incident of how Manibhadra had acquired gold using the same technique. So Manibhadra was also summoned to the court. Manibhadra told the judge about his dream. Finding the barber guilty, the judge sentenced him to death, saying: "*Before doing any work, a man should thoroughly investigate the negative and positive aspects, otherwise he will regret it* like the Brahmin."

Insight: Study all aspects of a problem before acting upon it. Otherwise, the solution will be worse than the problem. Imitating others blindly can have disastrous consequences. A system that may have worked for one person, may not necessarily work for another.

Manibhadra asked about the story of the Brahmin. The judge then narrated the following tale:

The Brahmin's Wife and the Mongoose

There once lived a Brahmin called Dev Sharma. After he got married, his wife gave birth to a child in due course. At the same time, a female mongoose had delivered and died. The Brahmin's wife felt sorry for the baby mongoose and decided to look after it. She even gave it her milk to drink, looking after it as if it were her own son.

One day, the Brahmin's wife went to fetch water after instructing the Brahmin to take care of the child. After some time, the Brahmin went away to seek alms, leaving the child alone. In the meantime, a black cobra entered the house. Spotting his enemy, the young mongoose was very angry. He fought with the cobra and ultimately killed him. The mongoose was very happy that he had saved the life of his brother (the Brahmin's child). He waited for the Brahmin or his wife to return, standing proudly at the door.

When the Brahmin's wife returned, she saw the mongoose's mouth smeared with blood. Immediately, she jumped to the conclusion that the mongoose had killed her son. In blind anger, she smashed the water pot she was carrying on the mongoose's head. The mongoose died instantly. When she entered the house, she was surprised to find her child playing happily on the cot. A dead cobra lay under the cot. In a flash, she registered everything and began to wail in grief. She cursed herself for killing the mongoose who had saved her son's life.

Insight: Don't take any hasty action before checking out where you stand. If you do so, whether in personal or professional life, you may regret it forever. Only when you analyse the situation will you be able to decide on the right course of action.

When the Brahmin returned, his wife blamed him for the mongoose's death: "It is only because of your greed that our foster son, the mongoose, died. I had warned you against going anywhere, but you were enslaved by greed and did not heed my advice. Didn't you know that a man possessed by excessive greed has a spinning wheel on his head?"

The Brahmin asked what she was talking about. His wife then narrated the following story:

Chakradhar – the Greedy Man

There once lived four Brahmin friends who, despite their learning, were very poor. Finally, they were tired of their penury and decided to move to another country to earn money. They reached Ujjayini. After taking bath in the river Shipra, they visited the Mahakaleshwar temple.

As they were coming out of the temple, they met a hermit named Bhairwanad and accompanied him to his hermitage. After treating his guests, the hermit asked: "Where have you come from and where do you want to go?"

They replied: "We are poor Brahmins. We want to acquire wealth. We have decided that either we will become wealthy or give up our lives."

They sought his help in this regard. Bhairwanad then gave them four lamps whose wicks were blessed with the powers of a mantra and said: "Go towards the Himalayas and walk until the wicks of your lamps begin to fall one by one. Dig at the place where the wicks of your lamps fall and you will find wealth."

The four friends proceeded towards the Himalayas with the lamps. After some time, the wick of one of the lamps fell down. All of them dug up the place and were amazed to find a copper mine. The first Brahmin told his friends to take all the copper, but they refused. So he took as much copper as he could carry and returned home.

The remaining three friends proceeded further. After travelling for some time, the wick of the second friend's lamp fell down. They dug up the place and found a silver mine. The second Brahmin asked his friends to take all the silver. But they refused, thinking that first it was copper, then silver, so may be they would strike gold the third time. The second Brahmin took as much silver as he could carry and turned back.

Now only two Brahmins were left. They proceeded further. Soon, the wick of the third lamp fell down. Both dug up the place and were amazed to find a mine of gold. The third Brahmin asked his friend to take all the gold, but the latter refused, anticipating jewels in his mine. So the third Brahmin took as much gold he could carry and prepared to return. The fourth Brahmin requested him to go along with him, but the third refused, saying: "I will wait for you here. Go and try your luck."

The fourth Brahmin proceeded alone. After walking some distance, he found an injured man lying on the ground, with a wheel spinning over him. He went near the man: "Who are you? How did you get injured? And why is this wheel spinning over your head?"

Hardly had the fourth Brahmin finished his words, when the wheel left the injured man and stuck to his head. The injured man replied that just like him, he too had gone in search of gold, found an injured man and asked him the same question: "Since then, the wheel had been spinning over my head. Now your misery will only end when a man arrives here with a desire for wealth."

Saying this, the injured man disappeared, while the fourth Brahmin remained there with the wheel spinning over his head.

Now the third friend who had discovered gold was still waiting for the fourth Brahmin. When he did not turn up even after many days, the third Brahmin was worried and went in search of the fourth.

Reaching the place, he found the fourth friend lying injured, with a wheel spinning over his head and asked how this had happened.

The fourth friend narrated the entire story. The third said: "Intelligence has greater value than learning or knowledge. Even qualified people lacking in intelligence are destroyed like the Brahmins who knew how to bring a dead lion back to life."

Insight 1: Working together, rather than individually, will help you attain your goals more easily.

Insight 2: The three places where the men struck gold, silver and copper probably had enough to make the entire city wealthy, yet the fourth man did not know the limits of greed. Ambition is good but the dividing line between ambition and greed is critical. Good fortune can be pushed only up to a point and not beyond. Only a mature mind can recognise where ambition ends and greed begins.

The fourth friend, whose name was Chakradhar, asked the third friend, Suvarnasiddhi, to narrate the story of the lion that was brought back to life. Suvarnasiddhi narrated this tale:

The Lion and the Foolish Brahmins

Four Brahmins who were very good friends once lived in a village. While three were great scholars, the fourth was illiterate but had lots of practical knowledge.

One day, all the friends decided to visit another country to earn money. However, one of them decided not to give anything to the fourth friend from whatever he received from the king, saying: "He is not a scholar and has not read any Scriptures. He has only some practical knowledge, which does not entitle him to rewards from the king."

So the second friend advised the fourth to turn back, as he was not a scholar.

The third, however, convinced the others to allow him to accompany them, saying: "Friends! He too is our friend! We must not abandon him like this."

All of them then agreed to take him along and proceeded on their journey. As they were passing a forest, they saw some bones on the ground and decided to test their knowledge. One collected the bones and erected the skeleton through the powers of his mantra. The second added flesh, skin and blood to the skeleton through the powers of his mantra. As the third friend was about to infuse a new lease of life into the animal through the powers of his mantra, the fourth friend said: "Stop! This is a lion. Do not resurrect it, because it will kill all of us."

All the friends laughed at him, saying he was being unduly concerned and that they would certainly test their knowledge.

When the fourth Brahmin realised his friends were adamant on resurrecting the lion, he climbed a tree to save his life. As soon as the lion was brought back to life, he devoured all the three Brahmins. When the lion went away, the fourth Brahmin came down the tree and quickly returned home.

Insight: Theoretical knowledge without practical abilities and common sense is useless and even harmful. To exploit scientific/ technical knowledge you also need to know how to control it. Or it will control you. Everything you create, whether goods or the market for your goods, must be such that you find it manageable. Goods you cannot market will ruin you and a market you cannot service will destroy you like the lion destroyed three of the four Brahmins.

The Foolish Wise Men

Four friends who lived in a village once decided to go to another place and seek education. The very next day they embarked on their journey and reached a city called Kanyakubja. There they gained admission in a school and studied for twelve years. They were now scholars of high standing.

One day they decided to return to their village. As they were returning, they reached a spot where the path divided into two and were confused as to which path they should follow. Undecided, they sat down at that very place.

Soon, a funeral procession arrived. One of the friends quickly took out a book and found a line that said: "One should follow the path trodden by many people."

The four friends then decided to accompany the funeral procession. When it finally reached the cremation ground, they saw a donkey standing there.

The second friend then produced his book, opened it and found a line that said: "Only that man can be considered a friend who accompanies one in celebration, in calamities, during famine, while surrounded by enemies, in the royal court and at the cremation ground."

Considering the donkey their friend, one of them embraced it and another washed its feet. Just then they saw a camel. The third friend opened his book and found a line saying: "The speed of religion is very fast."

The camel was walking swiftly, so the friends thought it to be a religion. The fourth friend said: "Let us join our friend with the religion."

The donkey was tied to the camel. Somebody conveyed this to the washer, who owned the donkey. He came running with a stick in his hand. Seeing the washer coming in hot pursuit, the four friends fled.

Later, they arrived at a riverbank, where they saw a leaf floating on the water. One of them thought the leaf was sinking. So he jumped into the river to save the leaf, having heard the proverb that a sinking man even clings to a straw. Since he did not know how to swim, he began drowning and cried for help.

The third friend opened his book and found a line saying: "When there is a possibility of losing everything, one must try to save half, because the grief of losing everything is unbearable."

The third friend beheaded the drowning one, thinking that thus he would save at least half of his friend. Now only three of them survived.

They proceeded further and reached a village. The villagers mistook them for learned scholars and invited them to their homes. One of them was offered vermicelli (*sevai*). He thought that a *Deerghasutri* (one with long thread-like worms) is doomed to die, so he did not eat the *sevai*, fearing he would die.

The other friend was offered bread. He thought that an excessively expanded object is impermanent. He did not eat the bread fearing premature death. The last friend was offered *bada* (ground pulse formed into small round cakes and fried), but found the *bada* porous. He thought that things with small pores invite calamities; hence he did not eat it. In this way the three foolish friends returned home starving.

Insight: Book learning is useless if you lack common sense. You need a feel of the real world and practical knowledge, before you can utilise your theoretical knowledge. In other words, street smartness is required to find prospective clients and reach them. Simply arming yourself with a management degree may not help. If you cannot relate what you study to the real world, it will not be of practical use.

After completing his story, Suvarnasiddhi told Chakradhar that the lack of practical knowledge was the reason for his miseries.

But Chakradhar disagreed, saying: "This happened only because of my destiny. If destiny is unfavourable, even a learned man faces hardships. But if destiny is favourable, even a foolish man enjoys life richly."

Suvarnasiddhi wondered how a foolish man could enjoy life thus. Chakradhar narrated the following story:

Insight: There may be a lucky few for whom destiny has kept something great in store. But usually even these people have to make the right moves to attract luck on their side. Without developing commendable rapport with the world even the 'destined' luck could bounce back right from your door.

The Fish and the Frog

Two fish named Shatabuddhi and Sahastrabuddhi once lived in a pond. Both developed friendship with a frog called Ekabuddhi. One day some fishermen arrived at the lake and were pleased to see the low level of water. So they decided to return the next day to catch some fish.

All the fish and the frog were terrified. The frog told Shatabuddhi: "Did you hear what the fishermen said? What should we do now? Can we continue living here or should we go to some other lake?"

Sahastrabuddhi laughed at the frog: "We must not believe the fishermen merely because of what they said. They are not going to come. Even if they come, I will protect you."

Shatabuddhi had complete faith in Sahastrabuddhi's intelligence and said: "We must not be scared of garrulous people."

Despite this, the frog migrated to another lake with his family. The next day, the fishermen arrived, sprang their net and caught many fish. Shatabuddhi and Sahastrabuddhi too were caught. Both tried their best but could not free themselves from the net.

One fisherman carried Shatabuddhi and Sahastrabuddhi on his shoulder. As he was passing by the lake into which the frog had moved the

previous night, the frog noticed Shatabuddhi and Sahastrabuddhi and said: *"A haughty man who lacks practical knowledge meets the same end as Sahastrabuddhi."*

After completing his story, Suvarnasiddhi admonished Chakradhar: "You did not pay any heed to my warnings because of excessive greed and pride in your knowledge. Somebody has rightly said: 'O uncle! Do not sing.' I made this request so many times but still you did not heed my advice. Now you have received a prize for singing a song, in the form of a beautiful diamond tied around your neck!"

Insight: We must have the humility to learn from the advice of the experienced as they possess more practical knowledge. At the very least, we should be courteous enough to find out the reason for their advice, rather than combating them with our arguments. Once you understand the logic behind the advice, you may find it easier to heed.

Chakradhar could not understand what he was saying, so he requested Suvarnasiddhi to elucidate.

Suvarnasiddhi narrated the following tale:

The Jackal and the Donkey

A washer once had a donkey named Uddhat, whose life was very hard. After toiling the whole day for his master, the donkey would roam about at night foraging green grass, returning to his master's house early every morning.

One night the donkey met a jackal. Both became friends. The jackal guided the donkey to a fenced field where juicy cucumbers grew and expressed his desire to eat the cucumbers. Being strong and healthy, the donkey broke the fence easily and both sneaked into the field. There they had their fill of juicy cucumbers. Thereafter, this became their daily routine.

Once, finding the moonlit night very beautiful, the donkey expressed his desire to sing, while they were in the cucumber field. The prospect of the donkey singing frightened the jackal as he was sure that if the donkey did so, his braying would attract the farmer. The jackal tried to dissuade the donkey, but the latter was adamant, saying: "You do not know anything about music. Even the deities love music. Even Ravana, the demon king, had pleased Lord Shiva with his songs."

When the jackal realised the donkey was hell-bent on singing, he slid out of the cucumber field, saying: "I will listen to your song from a distance."

The donkey then began singing. Hearing this, the farmer came rushing with a stick in hand and thrashed the donkey severely. The foolish donkey fell down and the farmer tied a wooden mortar around his neck, to prevent the donkey from fleeing, and himself went back to sleep.

After some time, the donkey fled with the wooden mortar still tied to his neck. When the jackal saw him fleeing, he said: "O uncle! I had warned you against singing, but you did not listen. You have received a beautiful diamond as your reward, which is hanging down your neck."

Insight: Stubbornness coupled with ignorance about the basics can make a doubly dangerous combination of personal characteristics, which will undermine whatever leadership qualities you have. Avoid them at all costs. Even if your activities are laudable and will please the boss, there is a right time and a right place for everything; unless you realise this, all may be lost.

After Suvarnasiddhi had finished his story, Chakradhar agreed and said: "If an unintelligent person does not pay heed to the advice of his friends, he is sure to meet the same fate as that of Manthar the weaver."

Suvarnasiddhi asked about the story of Manthar. Chakradhar narrated the following tale:

Manthar – the Weaver

A weaver named Manthar once lived in a village, earning his livelihood weaving clothes. While at work one day, his spinning wheel broke down. As the only means of his livelihood was destroyed, he became sad. He then decided to earn his livelihood by selling wood.

So he went to the seashore with an axe in hand. There he saw a huge rosewood tree and decided to axe it. A Yaksha who lived on this tree requested Manthar not to cut it down. But Manthar did not pay heed and asked the Yaksha to move to some other tree. "I can earn a lot of money by selling the wood of this big tree," said Manthar.

The Yaksha realised he was very poor and said: "I am pleased by your innocence. I can fulfil one wish of yours."

Very happy, Manthar requested the Yaksha to wait until he returned after asking his wife what to demand. The Yaksha agreed. As Manthar was walking home, he met his barber friend. He told him everything about the Yaksha and asked what he should demand. The barber advised him to ask for an empire. "You will be the king and I will be your minister," said the barber.

Manthar liked the idea, but still went to ask his wife. At home, he narrated the story to her and also mentioned what the barber had suggested.

Manthar's wife told him: "Your friend does not know the troubles a king faces ruling over his subjects. Even his queen is burdened with tension. Your occupation is best for you. But there is one problem. You can do very little work with two hands. Ask for two extra hands to do more work. And don't forget to ask for an extra head."

Manthar returned to the Yaksha and expressed his desire to have four hands and two heads. After the Yaksha granted his desire, Manthar returned to his village happily. As he was entering the village, the villagers mistook him for a demon and killed him.

Insight: Ambition is laudable as long as it does not turn you into a moral monster. The dividing line between ambition and greed is nebulous and crossing this could bring you grief.

Completing his story, Chakradhar said: "One who worries about the accomplishment of impossible tasks suffers from jaundice just like the father of Somsharma."

Suvarnasiddhi asked: "How did this happen?"

Chakradhar narrated the following tale:

Somsharma's Father

There once lived a very miserly Brahmin who collected whatever he got as alms in an earthen pot and kept this hanging right over his bed, guarding it jealously.

Lying in his bed one night, he thought: 'If a famine hits the city, I will sell my grains at a high price. With that money I will purchase many goats. After selling the goats, I will purchase cows. After selling the cows, I will purchase buffaloes. After selling the buffaloes, I will purchase mares. They will certainly litter and there will be many more horses and mares. Then I will sell them and purchase gold. I will then have my own house and get married to an extremely pretty woman.

'After marriage I will become the proud father of a son. I will name my son Somsharma. When Somsharma starts crawling, I will sit in a stable with a book in my hand to test his intelligence. Seeing me sitting in the stable, Somsharma will try to crawl near me.

'I will order my wife to hold Somsharma, but because of many household chores, she will not listen to me. I will then kick her.'

Thinking thus, the Brahmin kicked the earthen pot violently and it broke into pieces shattering all his dreams to smithereens.

Insight: A person who worries about unnecessary things faces sorrow. Excessive and unnecessary planning for the future clouds the present. Besides, planning for a happy future cannot include the infliction of cruelty on another. The fulfilment of your dreams will depend partly on how positive and sensible they are. Likewise, in professional life, your prosperity plans must exclude any underhand plots against competitors. If energy is channellised in a negative direction, there won't be much left to grow prosperous.

After completing his story, Suvarnasiddhi said: "A man who in his restlessness does work without thinking about the consequences gets betrayed just like Chandrabhupati."

Chakradhar wanted to know how Chandrabhupati was betrayed. Suvarnasiddhi narrated the following story:

The Monkey's Revenge

There once lived a king named Chandrabhupati, who had many monkeys in his palace. The leader of the troop was an old but very intelligent monkey, Ushanas.

There were many sheep in the palace too, on whose backs the princes enjoyed riding. One of the sheep was extremely naughty, entering the kitchen whenever it had the chance and devouring whatever it found. Whenever the cook saw this sheep in the kitchen, he hit it with any utensil within reach.

One day, Ushanas saw the cook hitting this sheep. He thought their enmity was certain to cause problems for the monkeys some day. He expressed his feelings to the other monkeys, but nobody listened to him. Ushanas again tried to convince them: "Look! The cook hits the sheep with anything he finds. One day, when he finds nothing, he will hit the sheep with a burning stick. The fleece of the sheep will surely catch fire. The sheep will then run towards the stable to extinguish the fire. The grass and straw kept in the stable will catch fire. The horses will be severely burnt. The burn injuries will only heal by applying the fat of a monkey on the wound and the king will then kill all of us. So it will be better if we leave this place at once and retire to the forest."

All the monkeys laughed at Ushanas and derided him, saying he had grown senile. Ushanas then left the palace along with his family.

One day what Ushanas had predicted happened. The cook flung a burning stick at the sheep and the fleece caught fire. The sheep fled

towards the stable, which was soon engulfed in flames. Many horses were burnt. The king called the physician, who prescribed the fat of monkeys as medication. The king then ordered the slaughter of all the palace monkeys.

Insight: Preventive action saves unpleasantness. Only an intelligent and mature person acquires the foresight to anticipate catastrophe and formulate ways to prevent it. If we heed their warnings, much heartache can be avoided. Instead, if we laugh them off as paranoid, we may even have to pay the ultimate price for ignoring their farsightedness.

When Ushanas learnt about the incident, he felt very angry and vowed to avenge the slaughter of his tribe.

One day, while Ushanas was wandering in a forest feeling thirsty, he reached a lake. As he was about to enter the water, he noticed footmarks entering the lake. However, there were no footmarks going away from the lake. Ushanas sensed something amiss. He decided not to enter the lake and drank water through the hollow stem of a lotus plant.

A demon lived inside the lake, who was very pleased with Ushanas's intelligence and told him: "Ask for any boon."

Ushanas enquired about the demon's strength and he replied: "My strength is unmatched inside the water, but outside even a jackal could defeat me."

Ushanas had noticed that the demon was wearing a diamond necklace around his neck and said: "If you give your diamond necklace to me, I can bring the entire family of the king to you. This way both of us will fulfil our objectives."

Believing his words, the demon gave his diamond necklace to the monkey. Ushanas then went near the king's palace and began jumping from one tree to another.

When the soldiers saw such a strange monkey, they informed the king: "Maharaj! There is a monkey wearing a beautiful diamond necklace, which even we do not have in our palace."

Ushanas was summoned and the king enquired about the necklace. Ushanas replied: "There is a lake in the forest. Anyone who takes a bath in this lake is presented with a necklace."

The king immediately went to the lake with the queen and the princes. Ushanas too accompanied them. When they reached the lake, Ushanas advised the king to let the queen and the princes have their bath first. The king agreed. The queen and the princes went into the lake to take their bath.

When they did not return from the lake after a while, the king asked the monkey about this. The monkey quickly climbed up a big tree and replied: "O king! Your family will never come back from the lake because they have been devoured by the demon living in the lake. I have taken my revenge. I spared your life because I want you to suffer in the same manner as I am suffering."

Insight 1: All actions that are self-centred and ignore the well-being of others are likely to meet with untoward consequences. Was the slaughter of all the monkeys necessary?

Insight 2: One black sheep turned out to be disastrous for the entire palace. Any black sheep tendencies at the place you work should be nipped in the bud. If left unchecked, your flock or even the entire company could eventually crumble.

After finishing his story, Suvarnasiddhi expressed his desire to return home. Chakradhar requested him to help him come out of his miserable condition, but Suvarnasiddhi wanted to leave the place as soon as possible, lest he himself be ensnared in some distress. He said: "The expression on your face resembles that of the thief who was haunted by a demon. Only those who run away from here can survive."

Chakradhar asked about the story of the thief haunted by a demon.

Suvarnasiddhi narrated the following tale:

The Monkey and the Demon

A king named Bhadrasen had an extremely beautiful daughter. A demon called Vikal was infatuated with her beauty and tormented the princess every night.

One night, while the princess was narrating her woes to a friend, Vikal arrived suddenly. When he heard the princess, he thought she was talking about some other demon. Frightened of this imaginary demon, he disguised himself as a horse and hid in the stable.

In the night, a thief entered the stable to steal a horse. He chose Vikal as he looked very healthy. Reining the horse, the thief mounted him. Now Vikal was very frightened. He thought the thief was the same demon whom the princess had mentioned. The thief then whipped the horse to get him going. Vikal was certain the person riding him was none other than the demon, so he galloped away in terror. The thief tried to stop him by pulling the reins, but Vikal in the horse's guise did not break his stride.

Now the thief was afraid. He realised the horse he was riding was a demon, in reality. As Vikal passed under a banyan tree, the thief grabbed one of its branches and somehow climbed up the tree.

A monkey lived on the banyan tree, who was a friend of Vikal, the demon. He recognised Vikal in the guise of a horse and said: "Amazing! Instead of eating this man you are running away from him terrified!"

The thief was more terrified and bit the monkey's tail. The monkey thought the thief was more powerful than Vikal and, dumbstruck with terror, his eyes closed.

When Vikal saw the monkey become speechless, he thought perhaps the monkey too had been possessed by the demon. Frightened out of his wits, he fled never to return again.

Insight: Baseless fear can cloud your judgement with fatal consequences. If the fear is overwhelming (as was the demon's) your mental abilities could get so numbed you could fear your own shadow – just as it happened with this demon when he heard his own description from the lips of the princess.

Observation: *The innocent princess inadvertently secured her revenge against the demon without debasing her heart with hatred. The demon's evil attracted the punishment it deserved. Likewise, if we fill our mind with negative thoughts and emotions, we will only attract negativity. Conversely, if we think and act positively at all times, the good things in life are more likely to come our way.*

After completing his story, Suvarnasiddhi told Chakradhar: "Even if a man knows everything, he must still be curious because a Brahmin possessed by a demon could save his life only because of his curiosity."

Chakradhar wanted to know the story of the curious Brahmin.

Suvarnasiddhi narrated the following tale:

The Brahmin and the Demon

A Brahmin once lived in a region surrounded by forests, which was also home to a demon. One day the demon found the Brahmin wandering alone and at once sat on the Brahmin's shoulder and ordered him to move forward.

The Brahmin was very afraid and followed the demon's command helplessly. The Brahmin noticed that the demon's feet were very soft and curiously enquired about this.

The demon replied: "I have taken a vow that I will not touch the ground with my wet feet."

The Brahmin was thinking of a plan to free himself from the clutches of the demon. As the Brahmin passed by a lake, the demon expressed his desire to have a bath. He instructed the Brahmin to stay there until he returned from his bath. The demon then went to take his bath.

The Brahmin knew that after his bath, the demon would certainly devour him. Suddenly, he remembered the demon's vow. So he ran away knowing fully well that the demon would not chase him with wet feet.

132

After completing his story, Suvarnasiddhi said: "A task which is accomplished without consensus causes destruction in the same manner as a bird named Bharund was destroyed."

Chakradhar wanted to hear the story of Bharund. Suvarnasiddhi narrated the following tale:

Bharund – the Bird With Two Heads

On the shore of a lake there once lived a strange bird called Bharund. He had one stomach but two heads and two mouths.

One day, Bharund was eating a delicious fruit with one of his mouths and simultaneously describing its taste. The other mouth too wanted to taste the delicious fruit, but the first mouth refused the request saying: "We both have a common stomach, so where is the need of your tasting this food? It would be better if I gave the remaining portion of this fruit to my wife."

The next day, the second mouth got some poisonous food. He told the first mouth he wanted to eat the poisonous fruit. The first mouth said: "Do not eat this fruit, else both of us will die."

Being angry with the first mouth for not giving it the sweet fruit, the second mouth did not pay heed to this advice and ate the poisonous fruit. As a result, both of them died.

After completing his story, Suvarnasiddhi again expressed his desire to go home. Chakradhar agreed but advised him not to go alone because a Brahmin could save his life only because of Karkat who was accompanying him.

Suvarnasiddhi asked: "How did this happen?"

Chakradhar narrated the following story:

The Brahmin and the Crab

A Brahmin named Brahmadutt lived in the city. One day, he decided to go to another city for some work. His mother asked who was accompanying him. He replied that he was going alone. Brahmadutt's mother advised him to take somebody along, as *having a companion is very useful while travelling.*

Brahmadutt's mother gave him a crab and said: "This crab will be your companion on this journey."

Brahmadutt proceeded on his journey with the crab, which he kept inside a small camphor box. In the afternoon, he decided to take rest under the shade of a tree. Being tired he soon fell asleep. While he was sleeping a snake emerged from the hollow of that tree.

The snake was attracted by the smell of the camphor box and tried to swallow it. The crab came out from the box and killed the snake.

When Brahmadutt woke up from his sleep, he found a dead snake lying near the camphor box. He realised that the crab had saved his life.

Insight 1: One should never underestimate anyone's usefulness. Even a small creature such as a crab that could not talk, and was unable to even awaken Brahmadutt and warn him of impending danger, proved to be a great companion by saving his life.

Insight 2: Parents and elders are more experienced and wiser than us. Therefore, almost always, their advice is bound to be useful.

Conclusion

Five Leadership Secrets from the Panchatantra

The leadership secrets taught by the five tantras are:

1. Avoid rifts with friends, colleagues, associates, clients and whoever you deal with. They can only lead to unpleasant consequences. As a leader, try to be a peacemaker, doing your best to patch up quarrels between those within your purview.

2. Try to make as many friends as possible by joining professional associations and trade bodies, where you can learn invaluable lessons and gain experience from associates.

3. Learn not to trust those who have proved their unreliability through actions and unworthy behaviour.

4. Cultivate presence of mind under all circumstances by following role models who possess these qualities and learn how they do it.

5. Learn to operate in untested situations as they develop. Experience will help you deal with situations you are unfamiliar with. The creativity and experience of your team of friends, colleagues and associates who have faced similar situations will help you deal with them.

You can merge these five ancient leadership secrets with the five steps in modern management to become a successful leader:

1. Plan: Determine your goal and target. Decide which methods you will adopt to reach them.

2. Do: Acquire the learning and training you need to implement your plan.

3. Check: Check the effects of your implementation.

4. Action: Take counter-action to remedy mistakes and prevent future errors.

5. Move on to the next plan.

To sum up, think ancient and act modern in order to survive and thrive in a rapidly changing world.

Solve Your Problems —The Birbal Way

—Luis S.R. Vas & Anita S.R. Vas

***Over 85 amusing and
engrossing tales to spark
your creative thinking***

Unravelling in the Court of Akbar, the well-known Birbal stories illustrate the minister's sagacity and problem-solving acumen.

It has become trendy to identify various management and leadership styles with historical and mythical personalities such as Attila the Hun, Winnie the Pooh, Mulla Nasruddin, Confucius and Jesus Christ, and with philosophical systems and religious books like Zen, Taoism, the Kabballah, the Bible, the Bhagavad Gita and Sufism. Against this backdrop, the authors thought it would be appropriate to unveil the managerial wisdom and problem-solving principles that Birbal's stories embody.

They have retold some of the Birbal stories that they gathered and at the end of each they have pointed out the Management Moral of the narrative, whose wisdom remains as fresh as ever. They have divided each story into two parts. The first part consists of the problem; the second part provides Birbal's solution.

Readers are encouraged to pause just before the solution is given and think of their own solution to the problem. Only when they have thought of one or more solutions should they read Birbal's solution. There is no more effective way of honing one's own creativity.

At the end of the book, the authors have devised a technique that they have termed BIRBAL (an acronym) and which readers can use to solve their problems.

Demy Size • Pages: 200
Price: Rs. 80/- • Postage: Rs. 15/-

Skills for Excellence

— *Luis S.R. Vas*

How do you achieve excellence in a world of growing complexity and rapid technological change? The first step is a thirst for excellence. This is the motivation to achieve quality in whatever you do. Around the world numerous consultants have combined insights from behavioural sciences to train people in achieving excellence in various realms. But excellence requires skills in various areas.

In **Skills for Excellence** the author has brought together within one volume most of the ideas and practices which are being taught in enterprises around the world. The book starts with achievement motivation and shows how, as research has proved, this skill can be cultivated and developed. The other skills presented in this book are innovativeness drawn from the ideas of Peter Drucker and others; thinking skills from the concepts developed by Edward de Bono; a problem-solving technique devised by Rudolf Flesch; creativity as taught by Robert Fritz.

There are also time management, learning ability, communication skills and your retention powers. An equally basic but often neglected skill is the ability to maintain your health and fitness. All these skills are covered at length adapting ideas from masters in their respective fields.

Demy Size • Pages: 176
Price: Rs. 88/- • Postage: Rs. 15/-

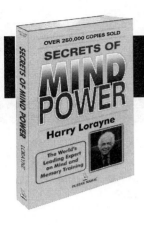

SECRETS OF MIND POWER

—Harry Lorayne

Do you want to be successful?
Are you ready to improve yourself?
Looking for a better and happier life?

Of course the answer is YES! You have the desire and now, here are the ways by which you can achieve these goals. With Harry Lorayne's proven methods — from the world's foremost authority on memory training — you will learn how to organize and develop the hidden powers of your mind!

This is the first revised edition of the famous bestseller, *Secrets of Mind Power*. It is Lorayne's 14th book on the subject of memory. You are treated to the proven techniques and methods of a professional, as you are shown how to use your mind to its fullest capacity.

Here is a sample of the benefits you will receive:

❖ Increasing your powers of memory and concentration
❖ Strengthening good habits and discarding bad ones
❖ Becoming an effective public speaker
❖ Conquering fear
❖ Taking on a new attitude and approach to life
❖ Improving your powers of observation
❖ Making friends easily and quickly
❖ Thinking logically, effectively and creatively
❖ Learning to trust others
❖ Becoming more organized and time-efficient

Demy Size • Pages: 184
Price: Rs. 96/- • Postage: Rs. 15/-

SUCCESS SECRETS
A Common Sense Guide to Life Long Achievement

—Merrill Douglass

This is the success secrets seminar you've been looking for!

Outstanding success is now within your reach — the keys to achieving it are in your hands! *Success Secrets* gives you *all* the powerful, life-changing guidance and direction you need to reach your full potential in your personal and professional life.

These dynamic success secrets won't just help you get to the top of your field, they'll enable you to get more of everything you want — on the job, in your relationships, and even in your leisure time. You'll master dozens of expert techniques for:

❖ managing your time
❖ setting reachable goals
❖ presenting a professional image
❖ getting ahead in your career
❖ leading effectively
 and much more!

Internationally-known speaker and time-management seminar leader, Dr. Merrill Douglass, delivers your keys to success in concise mini-chapters that are easy to read even on your busiest days! You'll turn to them again and again for quick reference, challenging direction, and uplifting encouragement.

A world-class course in achievement, this collection of super-motivating secrets will help you reach and exceed your loftiest dreams! You don't need a seminar on success. All you really need is *Success Secrets*.

Demy Size • Pages: 256
Price: Rs. 120/- • Postage: Rs. 15/-

How to Motivate Others

to turn them into super performers

—Kurt Hanks

A Manager's Guide for productive management

If you are asked to lead a group or assigned to manage the affairs of an office, you will probably require some tools to succeed. The tool is motivation. Without motivation there is no success. No learning. No action. And, most important of all, without motivation there are no results. This book gives a modern and more effective approach to this age-old problem of lack of motivation. Each page is filled with new ideas, concepts, methods and approach. However, this book is only a tool box—the real solution comes when you effectively match and apply the ideas prescribed to the situation.

The book focuses on:

❖ The most workable formula for winning people to your way.
❖ How to move key people from where they are to where you want them to be.
❖ How to raise other's enthusiasm for your projects.
❖ What common little quirk causes more problems with other than any other and how you can avoid it.
❖ What you must see in others, that most people don't see, before you can get them to change.
❖ Secrets for dealing with stubborn people.
❖ How to make others take interest in your ideas.
❖ What everybody wants that you have.
❖ How to stop others from manipulating you.
❖ How to criticize without being resented.
❖ How to give orders that are followed effectively.
❖ How to get others to like you.
❖ How to get the ear of the key people in your organisation.

Big Size • Pages: 128
Price: Rs. 96/- • Postage: Rs. 15/-

Success Through
POSITIVE THINKING

—S.P. Sharma

Is half full better or half empty?
* Choose right
* Think better
* Live well

Present-day life has become too complex and complicated. There is a scramble for more and more. Money, power and wealth have become symbols of success and happiness. A confused sense of affairs and lopsided values, that's leading to a lot of tension and distress.

Now **Success Through Positive Thinking** shows you the way out, advocating a change of attitude through moderation, acceptance of things as they are, and inculcating of moral values. The result? A positive personality free of negative elements like anxiety, stress, greed, envy and jealousy!

An Overview

Success Through Positive Thinking shows you the right path to real happiness through:
* A proper perspective on life
* Meditation and prayers
* Importance of work
* Handling of criticism and slander
* Knowing the difference between right and wrong, real and unreal
* Proper channellising of sexual and physical energy.

Demy Size • Pages: 180
Price: Rs. 80/- • Postage: Rs. 15/-

10 Fundamental Rules of Success

—Carani N. Rao

10 definite steps and keys for creating your own success story

It is observed that throughout the majority of the classics of self improvement literature, there are 10 core steps or fundamental rules to achieve success which run as a common thread. The purpose of this book is to share with the readers, these 10 proven rules/principles or keys compiled from the vast ocean of success literature. Some of these essential rules include—(**setting a goal, positive mental attitude and self confidence, purposeful and burning desire, planning and preparation, resources, inputs, discipline, action, persistence or perseverance, prayer and values.**)

Here success is first defined; then the basic rules involved in achieving success are enumerated and explained with relevant anecdotes and stories. To these 10 fundamental rules, a set of success formulae as well as virtue capsules have also been added in the present book.

Pages: 128 • Price: Rs. 96/-
Postage: Rs. 15/-